Residential
Property Management

For agents, employees and owners

Bryan Law

Fox College of Business

First edition: May 2021

Fox College of Business

Disclaimer

Fox College of Business and Bryan Law are not engaged in rendering legal, accounting, real estate, or other professional services. This book should not be relied upon as providing such advice. We strongly urge that you seek professional advice prior to acting on the information contained herein.

The information contained herein has been obtained from sources which we believe are reliable, but we cannot guarantee its accuracy or completeness. Fox College of Business, Bryan Law, and every person involved in creating this book disclaim any warranty as to the accuracy, completeness, and currency of the contents of this book. We also disclaim all liability in respect of the results of any action taken or not taken in reliance upon information in this book.

Bryan Law BSc (Pure Maths), LLM, LLD

A well-known author, consultant, and educator in Canada, Bryan has a diversified professional background.

Bryan is a management consultant with more than 20 years of experience. He is also a legal researcher in various areas, including contract law, environmental law, human rights law, labour law, privacy law, and real estate law.

Different education institutions have hired Bryan to provide his business management, law, and real estate expertise. Bryan has authored over 20 books in various disciplines, including human rights, creative problem-solving, franchising, real estate, Feng Shui, employment law, and more.

Bryan's wide-ranging knowledge and professional experience, coupled with humorous presentation skills, have placed him in demand as a professional speaker as well.

Table of Contents

1. Introduction

The Need for the Profession

The landscape of real estate has changed a lot since the industrial revolution in the 19th century. More forms of real estate ownership and uses were created and developed. Initially, there were only farmlands, hotels, and small downtown business units for rent. All of them were managed by the owners. As more labourers were attracted to industrialized neighbourhoods, multi-unit buildings started to be built and rented out.

Initially, those rental buildings were small, usually not more than 40 units. Since the concept of incorporation or company formation was relatively new, most of the building owners were individuals. Those owners would manage the buildings themselves, even though they had other businesses or were employed in other fields.

The tasks to manage those small buildings were relatively simple as compared to the modern ones. The owners had to rent out the units, collect the rent, pay the superintendent or contractors to maintain the building, order the fuel and pay for the utilities and taxes. Although those tasks are still part of property management works today, they were relatively easy due to the straightforward tax rules, simple building features and materials used. Moreover, there were no laws to govern residential tenancies.

As the demand increased and the new inventions of building technologies, more extensive and higher buildings were constructed. It made leasing commercial and residential space to third parties a key business in modern cities and towns. On the other hand, more rules and regulations, such as the zoning bylaws, and commercial and residential tenancies laws, made property management a more sophisticated task than ever.

Now, commercial and residential real estate are two of the most popular investment tools in the market. They can generate steady monthly income plus significant appreciation in value over time. Some people classify the rental incomes generated from real properties are passive incomes, but some disagree. It is because passive income is defined as an income that requires no effort to earn and maintain, but real properties need maintenance and repair works, which are to be performed by owners or their contractors. Moreover, landlords need to communicate with their tenants about the issues regarding their tenancies. Therefore, real estate investment is not as passive as stocks and mutual funds in a way that the owners have to participate in the operations somehow.

Since the rental market size has become bigger and bigger, the scale of rental properties also becomes more considerable. Institutional investors replace many individual owners to become the key players in the market. They own large portfolios of investment properties. As a result, there are need to manage investment properties by professionals, either in-house or outsourced.

Types of Owners

The objectives of the owners will affect the quality and purpose of their property management. While most owners are profit-oriented individuals and corporations, many of them are non-profit organizations or government bodies. Their goals and objectives are different, together with different budgets. All of these will affect the property management style as well as its effectiveness. Common ownership types in the market include:

Sole Proprietorship

A sole proprietorship is a business entity, which is owned by one person, the sole proprietor. Basically, the business entity is the same as the sole proprietor, although the name may not be the same. For example, Leslie Doe may operate a company under the same name or a different name, say, Super Lucky Property Management. The rights and liabilities of the business fall into Leslie Doe alone and no one else.

A sole proprietor landlord owns the real property, reaps the benefits of any profits, but is personally and legally responsible for the debts and lawsuits related to the property. Sole proprietors are usually very dependent upon the property manager for guidance, as they all act alone and have to rely on the advice of professionals, including lawyers and accountants.

Partnerships

A partnership involves two or more parties pooling their capital to operate a company. It is a separate entity in terms of names, but the rights and liabilities also fall into the individual partners unless it is a limited partnership. The other type is called a general partnership, in which all partners have unlimited liabilities like the sole proprietors if the partners are individuals. In both types of partnerships, the company shares owned by partners can be uneven.

In a limited partnership, one or more partners are the general partners, and the others are limited partners. General partners can make decisions for the partnership, legally bind the business, and are personally liable for all the business's debts and obligations. Limited partners have limited liability, which is the capital they invested. Limited partners are also called silent partners because they cannot make decisions like the general partners do.

A partnership can be as big as a corporation. In some circumstances, a partnership can be formed by a number of corporations, including developers, financial institutions and investment funds.

Corporation

A corporation is a legal entity formed by single or multiple shareholders created under the law. "Corporation" has other names such as "Incorporated" and "Limited". The liability of a corporation is usually limited to its assets, and the shareholders are protected against personal liability in connection with the operation of the corporation.

A corporation is taxed at different corporate tax rates, typically less than the maximum tax rate for individuals. A corporation is subject to regulation in the jurisdiction that it is incorporated and the jurisdictions they carry on business.

When dealing with a corporation or partnership, it will be necessary for a property manager to check the active status and a list of directors of the corporation with a local registration office to ensure that it is a legal entity.

Non-profit and Government Agency

Non-profit organizations are legal entities organized and operated for public or social benefit. Their objective is not aiming to generate a profit for their owners. Like the public housing run by the governments or their agencies, non-profit housing projects, usually in the form of cooperatives, provide affordable residences to the grassroots level. Their main objective is to provide well-maintained and affordable homes to low- and moderate-income households instead of making profits.

Property managers who work for these owners must understand those owners' philosophies, core values, and goals. They may not want to increase the rents, or at least not to the allowed maximum limit; even doing so can improve the overall quality of the rental properties.

Types of Management

There are three main types of property management operations.

Agency Management

Many owners hire fee-based professional property management companies to manage their properties. Such management companies act as the owners' agents to rent out the units, collect rent, pay the bills and maintain the buildings. Such professional firms bring valuable experience and advanced technologies to their clients for better results. A property management contract must be signed between the property management company and the landlord to spell out the contract term, the duties of the manager and their fee.

Their fee is negotiable, usually a percentage of the net operating income of the property that they manage. It is a mutual benefit to use a percentage of the net operating income as the management fee. The primary goal for for-profit owners is to make a higher profit from the property, and net operating income is the profit before tax. If a property management company can increase its net operating income, its fee will also be increased. It is a win-win arrangement; the higher the net operating income, the happier the landlord and the property manager.

Agency management firms are usually big corporations and manage large portfolios of properties that belong to different clients. Since they have a large client base, they can enjoy benefits such as bulk purchase discounts, sophisticated software, blanket insurance policy and contracted onsite staffing. This type of property manager is an agent of the owners and owes the owners certain fiduciary duties. One of them is to protect the best interest of the property owners, which is also a natural "duty" of the in-house managers and self-managed owners below.

In-house Management

An in-house property management team is usually found in institutional organizations with an extensive property portfolio. Big landlords such as insurance companies, pension funds and large real estate investment companies usually have their own salaried property managers to manage their properties in-house.

The main reason for having an in-house property management team is that the owners believe it is more economical and efficient to hire property management professionals directly, under their control. That is true when they are large enough and can get the benefits of agency management. If the landlord is large enough, its in-house management team may provide the benefits mentioned in the above agency management section.

On the other hand, an in-house management team can be as small as a one-person team. It is because the corporation has only one or two properties to manage, probably their staff residence. In fact, many in-house management teams only manage properties for their own use, such as staff residences, offices and other self-use facilities. Universities have property managers to assist their facilities management team too.

Self-Management

Many owners, especially those of smaller buildings or individual dwellings, choose to manage the properties themselves. Some of them have other businesses or jobs to do, while some of them work as full-time property managers. Many of them do it as a semi-retirement job, especially when the building does not require frequent maintenance or attention. Although most of them are not professional property managers, many of them succeed in doing excellent jobs to improve the quality of the tenants and profit level. However, some of them are ruining their real estate investments by poorly managing their properties.

Since most owners are not trained professionals, they have limited experience and knowledge in property management. Many of them are not willing to work 'full-time" as they are retirees and want to travel at least a few times a year. Acting as a property manager will inhibit the freedom of the individuals to do so unless they have someone to back them up. Besides, the rise of tenants' desires and increased legal complexities in residential tenancies make it more difficult for amateurs to manage their own buildings. As a result, more and more owners turn to professionals to manage their properties for them.

2. Residential Specialty

Laypersons may think managing a residential property is the same as managing a commercial property. At least, some people believe all residential properties can be managed in the same way, or all owners have the same objective and mandate in property management. Others may think that the works of property managers are mainly leasing out the units and collecting rents. The duties of property managers are more than that.

Basic Duties

The management works can be as frequently as daily operations in retail malls, office buildings and large residential complexes where the landlords have to deal with the common areas that service the tenants and visitors. Moreover, visitors coming to the facilities every day and may have enquiries to be answered or issues that need to be solved. On the other hand, the frequency for a landlord to act can be just once a year or less. For example, a condominium unit owner who rents out the unit may only need to deal with the tenancy issues once a year or when the old tenant moves out and a new tenant moves in. While commercial property management is as crucial as the residential segment, this book will focus on the property management of residential properties.

Managing rental properties is a task that all owners must perform either by the property owners themselves or by third-party contractors. The term "property management" refers to the administrative operation and property maintenance based on the owner's objectives. The work involved may include daily operations and management plans designed to resolve serious property issues for a year or more to implement fully.

One of the property management objectives is to realize the maximum value of a building during its economic life. That is achieved by obtaining the maximum profit at the minimum costs and ensuring that the physical condition of the property is not compromised. Property management also needs to maintain a balance between responsibilities and services to owners and tenants. Landlord and tenant relation is, in fact, one of the interests that a property manager has to look after. The role of a professional property manager is similar to that of a financial advisor, with real estate as the specialty.

There are numerous duties for a property manager to fulfill, but we can group them into four areas in general. They are:

1. Keeping the property leased
2. Collecting property incomes
3. Paying the property expenses
4. Maintaining the property

Keeping the Property Leased

The rental market is dynamic. Tenants may terminate their tenancy at any time due to many reasons, such as relocation and financial issues. They may also simply not renew their lease. Whenever there is a vacant unit in the building, the property manager should rent it out at the market rent as soon as possible in order to maintain the rental income level.

A property manager has to pick good quality tenants to minimize vacancy and bad debt losses to obtain the highest possible rents. Therefore, a property manager should have the ability to forecast and interpret the supply and demand of the rental market. That is why property managers must be sensitive to market information to make sure their buildings are competitive.

Collecting Property Incomes

All rents are paid in advance unless there are exceptions. The rents received by a property manager may be reinvested, such in an interest-bearing account, to get more profits. Therefore, a property manager must collect all the rents on time. The landlord will not be released from the obligation of paying realty taxes, utilities and mortgage when a tenant does not pay rent. When a tenant is delinquent, the landlord may start losing money, so remedial measures must be taken.

There are regulations on how and when a notice of non-payment of rent is served in many jurisdictions. Property managers must be familiar with the requirements. If the notice of non-payment of rent is not served correctly, the property manager may not be able to evict the tenant according to the respective tenancy law.

Paying the Property Expenses

Paying the operating expense of the investment building is an essential task for a property manager. Often, the property manager may have to pay the mortgage payment for the owner using the rent received on behalf of the owner.

Paying the costs is just the minimum requirement. Property managers should find ways of minimizing operating costs, such as using energy-saving equipment, purchasing bulk orders, tendering services in advance, and paying utility and tax bills promptly to avoid late payment interests and penalties.

Maintaining the Property

Although a piece of land lasts forever, the building and other improvements erected on it are subject to wear and tear. Once the structures achieve their respective maximum age, they may have to be demolished. As a result, the owner may lose the rental income and need to reinvest the capital to rebuild them.

All those structures have two ages – actual age and effective age. Actual age is the number of years that have passed since a structure was built. It is also referred to as chronological age. Effective age is the estimated age in years based on the amount of care and attention a structure has received. Care and attention could include repair, replacement, renovation, and modernization. If a structure has had better than average maintenance, its effective age may be much less than its actual age. On the other hand, if there has been inadequate maintenance, its effective age may be much greater than its actual age.

Basic Tasks

As agents of the owners of properties, property managers have their primary responsibility owed to the owners and secondary responsibility to the tenants. Therefore, all the tasks performed by property managers should promote the owners' interest, including promoting the landlord-tenant relationship.

Bookkeeping

The tracking of receipts and disbursements is crucial for both owners and tenants, such as the proof of rent payments. Property managers must use appropriate bookkeeping forms, procedures and systems to record all the payments, especially where property management is a regulated profession.

Budgets

Budgeting is needed for every business, including the rental businesses operated by the owners and managed by property managers. There are two methods commonly used in the field. They are annual operating budgets and capital budgets. Bigger projects and institutional property managers will also perform monthly net operating income projections and monthly cash flow budgets.

Insurance

The property owners, property managers and real properties need various insurance coverages to protect them adequately. Following is a list of typical insurance coverages considered by property managers:

- Fire and extended coverage
- Comprehensive liability
- Boiler and machinery
- Multi-peril risks
- Catastrophe
- Rental income
- Error and omission (for the property managers)

Leases

Property managers will have to sign leases on behalf of the owners. Standard leases are usually drafted by the lawyer of the owner or the property management company. Sometimes they are supplied by the government where there is a law to stipulate a standard lease to be used. Owners and property managers may have their own rules and regulations on top of the laws unless they are disallowed by the local legislation.

Most residential leases are gross leases. The tenants pay a fixed rental amount, and the landlords pay all the expenses associated with the operating of the property. Typically, utility costs, parking costs, laundry facilities and extraordinary repairs are subject to negotiations between the landlords and tenants.

Maintenance Plan

Property managers must provide maintenance plans for the orderly upkeep of their managed properties. There are four steps involved in developing a plan. They are:

- Assessment of the needs
- Identification of the capabilities of onsite staff and equipment
- Estimation of the time that each maintenance job will take
- Rearrangement of the maintenance tasks according to resources

Security

Landlords are required to provide adequate security to their tenants; thus, property managers are expected to take reasonable measures to protect the tenants. The security system components should include consideration of hardware, design, personnel, and management elements. A well-designed plan must consist of all those aspects.

In addition to complying with legal requirements and safety arrangements, property managers can provide better security to improve the relationship between owners and tenants. Moreover, good communications and interactions among property managers, tenants and the onsite staff are essential to successful operations.

Types of Properties

Although many property managers may want to be specialized in particular areas to streamline their services, they can manage all types of residential properties in principle. Depending on the investor types, such as individual, institutional, non-profit or governmental, different properties are used as rental properties to accommodate the tenants.

Single Family Residential

Freehold houses and condominium units are the common investment type for small individual investors. They require less capital investment and are easier to sell. Freehold houses are in scattered locations which leads to higher servicing and maintenance costs. The lower density of such housing may also allow property managers to maintain a better landlord-tenant relationship.

Condominium buildings consist of both owner-occupied and tenanted units. Most jurisdictions have legislation to govern condominium complexes; hence, property managers may have to be licensed to comply with the laws. The property manager of a condominium will have to work with the board of directors of the condominium instead of the unit owners. Similar to condominiums, equity cooperative housing projects can be sold as investment units. Individual coop owners, like condominium owners, may rent out their units. The management requirements of cooperatives are similar to those of condominium buildings.

Multi-family Residential

Although a condominium complex has many units, it is not a multi-family residential building, as the units are owned by individual owners. A rental apartment building is a multi-family residential building because all the units in the rental building are owned by the same owner, and the units cannot be sold individually.

Non-profit cooperative and public housing projects are also typical multi-family residential buildings. Non-profit cooperative housing is developed by non-profit organizations to provide affordable rental housing to people while permitting resident members the opportunity to have a say in the upkeep and management of their residence. Public housing projects are run by the governments to provide affordable housing to the local residents.

All the above multi-family residential buildings have been structured for occupancy by a number of different households. As they provide only basic features, such as shared laundry facilities, the relationships among the tenants may cause problems. Non-profit cooperatives and public housing may have their own rules and regulations that are the prerequisites for people to be tenants. Those buildings may also be exempted from the residential tenancies law, which is mainly used to protect the tenants. Rental apartments have to have their own rules and regulations to deal with tenancy issues.

Multiplex

In between single-family houses and rental apartments, a multiplex is a residential building consisting of two or more self-contained units at ground level or built on multi-levels. All units have separate entrances. A multiplex is a good choice for investors who have limited capital to buy more significant investment projects. Especially, it is suitable for individuals who just have some degree of knowledge in property management and want to use it to practice their self-management skills.

A multiplex with only two units is called a duplex, and with three units is called a triplex. We have fourplex, five plex etc. There is no maximum number of units in a multiplex, although it is usually used to describe low-rise or medium-rise buildings with less than 100 units. For buildings with more than 100 units or high-rise buildings, they are just called rental apartments.

Retirement Communities

Retirement communities can be operated by for-profit and non-profit organizations too. They offer accommodation and various lifestyle options for active seniors. Retirement communities may consist of retirement homes and other facilities, such as condominium units for sale and commercial space. They typically include tenant and buyer selection restrictions such as age regarding occupancy.

Most retirement homes are rental properties and offer two levels of service, independent living and assisted living. Independent living is like living in a condominium, whereas assisted living is bundled with access to services like entertainment, housekeeping, personal support, healthcare, and meals. Residents of retirement communities will have to enter into a residency agreement setting out specifics of the accommodation and level of services provided. The costs of living vary mainly depending on the facilities and the level of service and support offered.

Mobile Homes

A mobile home is a portable dwelling unit that can be transported on its chassis, with or without its own running gear, and is designated to be used as a living quarter. By definition, a recreational vehicle can be a mobile home.

Mobile homes must be parked inside a mobile home park or a land lease community for long-term use in the cities. The landlord owns the land, structures, services and facilities for mobile homeowners to use as tenants. In many jurisdictions, mobile homes are specially treated under their residential tenancy laws.

Supply and Demand

Everyone needs shelter, but not everyone needs commercial space to run a business. Therefore, the vacancy rate of residential properties is the lowest among the others – office, retail, industrial and recreational. That is why the residential rental market is a relatively low-risk market for investors due to its nature. With the limited land supply to build residential dwellings, the value of residential properties will definitely appreciate over time, especially in the long run. That is why many investors are interested in investing in the residential rental market.

If the rental market performs well with rental rates increasing, more people will buy residential rental properties as investments. That will reduce the supply of all types of residential properties in the resale market. Developers may build more rental buildings and condominiums to accommodate the demand for residential properties.

However, there may be an over-supply if too many residential units are built simultaneously, which will adversely affect the rental market. Over-supply may also be caused by a decrease in demand.

The demand for residential rental units is a complex interplay of several factors, economic trends, unemployment, immigration, income level, and population age. When the economy is bad, more people will sell their homes, and rent a unit instead. If they are already renting, they may move to an area with lower living costs, leaving the original neighbourhood a higher vacancy rate. The same will happen when the unemployment rate goes up or the income level cannot catch up with the local inflation.

When more new immigrants come to the country, the demand for rental units increases because most new immigrants will rent first. Most of them will not buy their own house until they are settled. Retirement homes will be in demand when there are more seniors in society. On the other hand, a newly wedded couple will likely establish an independent household. That is known as a family formation. The newly married couple would look for another housing unit. Again, some of them will rent instead of buy. An increase in family formations typically creates an increase in demand for rental housing units.

If the demand for rental units is high, the vacancy rate will be low, and the rental rate will tend to increase subject to the rent controls in some jurisdictions. Conversely, if the demand is low, the vacancy rate will be high, and the property managers must reduce the rent to attract tenants.

Property managers should be sensitive to the residential rental market. The supply and demand in residential rental properties will affect the rental rates in the market, and the number of investors, rental units, and property managers required.

The typical approach to estimate the supply of rental properties involves analyzing the existing competition and new multi-residential buildings either currently approved or under construction. Sometimes, high-rise condominium buildings are also taken into consideration as they are also a good source of rental units.

Statistics are essential to study trends and market performance. Property managers should keep an inventory count of all buildings in the neighbourhood, including details such as the number of units in the building, the number of bedrooms in every unit, rent levels, basic features and services included, and the overall conditions of those buildings.

Suppose the buildings are close to the one that a property manager manages. In that case, more details should be recorded, such as the number of elevators (or just walk-up), exercise room, swimming pool, entertainment rooms and other party facilities. The locational features should also be included, such as the nearby parks, shopping centres, schools and transportation systems. Walkability is also crucial, especially for urban properties.

Requirements of Tenants

Why do people rent? That is the question that every property manager should ask. More specifically, the question is, "Why do people rent my property?"

There are several reasons for people to rent a property instead of buying one. It may be their economic change, change in the number of family members, change of work, marital status, retired, unemployed, or getting old, all leading to lifestyle changes. Tenants can be classified as either tenants by choice or tenants by necessity.

Tenants by Choice

Some people prefer renting to owning a property. People in this category are not obliged to rent for financial reasons. However, they choose to do so due to their particular lifestyle. Some of them are of an age when accommodation with a minimum demand of their time and effort is desirable, so they will rent a service apartment and save the cleaning works.

Some of them rent because of the proximity to the workplace, and the choice of buying is limited, or they need flexibility. Common types of tenants by choice include working couples with no kids, young professionals, seniors and singles.

Working couples with no kids include those in common-law relationships. Because of long working hours and demanding jobs, they have little time remaining for life enjoyment. Renting a furnished home, probably with housekeeping service, may minimize household chores, thereby maximizing leisure time. Another factor is that renting allows the couple to remain flexible and mobile without disposing of a residence. This kind of tenant will not take the school network into their consideration when picking rental properties.

The requirements for rental units of young professionals are similar to those of working couples with no kids. In particular, they will look for more entertainment establishments in the neighbourhoods, such as pubs, sports bars and theatres.

Seniors are retirees or semi-retirees who are close to retirement. They are the so-called "empty nesters" with children who married and moved out of their homes. The existing home may be too big for them. Since they are ageing, they may want to save energy on daily housekeeping and reduce their living costs. Renting can avoid paying property taxes and give them more cash flows. Some of them may want to move from a city to the countryside, so they may need short-term rentals before making the final decision. Seniors usually look for small apartments, retirement homes and assisted living housing.

People who are singles do not need too much space; many of them may choose small apartments to reduce the hassles of housekeeping. Since many singles prefer trying different kinds of jobs and like travelling, they may want to have the flexibility to move frequently. Renting allow them to be flexible and mobile without the task of selling a residence and buying a new one.

To conclude, all tenants by choice look for quality of life, so they also look for good quality rental housing.

Tenants by Necessity

Some people have to choose to rent a property instead of buying it. People in this category either have no option to purchase or must rent because of financial restrictions or other circumstances over which they have no control. Common types of tenants by necessity include families with kids, transients, people who rely on welfare and students.

Families with kids have a higher average cost of living than working couples with no kids. It is more difficult for single parents since there is usually only one source of income. For families with children, the costs of food, clothing, and other necessities leave a minimal amount for shelter, hence lowering their purchase power to buy a house. On the other hand, the real estate price continues to escalate and makes it difficult for them to arrange mortgage financing.

The jobs of some people require them to move from place to place on a short-term basis. They may be the employees of travel-related businesses, multinational management consulting firms, resource exploration companies and construction companies. Although they may be housed in temporary onsite buildings, they will seek accommodation in the nearest community to the project if they have spouses and families. The duration of their stay in rental housing will be short-term, usually less than a year.

Many people who rely on welfare do not own a house. With rare exceptions, their income is usually in the lower bracket. That makes them almost impossible to buy real properties. While some get public housing accommodations, some receive cash payments from the government instead of free housing. Those who receive cash payments will look for accommodation at a reasonable rent in the open market.

Many students who attend universities and colleges, especially international students, require accommodations as close to their campus as possible. While universities and colleges will offer residence on their campus, they are usually more expensive than private housing units. Students typically look for basic accommodation at the lowest possible rent, including co-living opportunities.

The majority of tenants by necessity are from the low-income class; many of them are unable to find affordable accommodation, depicting the desperate need for more non-profit and public housing.

The Owners

Property managers need to know the owner's intentions for the property to manage their properties effectively. That is important as it will impact the decisions of property managers regarding maintenance, repairs and tenant selection.

The goal of the owners of large rental properties is clear. The building is either for profit-generating purposes or non-profit purposes, including public housing. For smaller buildings, especially single-family residences, the reason for leasing out the property may be different.

A single-family residential property owner may purchase it as a revenue-producing investment, especially when they have a principal residence already, or the smaller property was purchased in a good market as a future retirement home. Sometimes, the property is inherited as part of an estate, and the owner wants to lease it while waiting for an improved market to sell it. Short-term leasing may also be an option for owners who have transferred to another city but wishes to retain the house and re-occupy it upon their return or retirement.

In general, the goal of the owners should not affect the quality of property management in any way. However, it will affect how property managers perform their works, such as the tenant selection process, rent increase process, and equipment investment.

According to the different goals of the owners, property managers have to adjust their leasing requirements to achieve the goals. For example, property managers have to determine the terms of their tenancies, whether they are long-term (such as at least one year term) or short-term (such as no fixed term). They will also decide if they want monthly or weekly tenancies. While most rental units are unfurnished, some are furnished with furniture, appliances, and even cooking utensils and linens.

Regardless of the type of building and the goals of the owners, property managers must perform specific tasks to fulfill their duties to the owners. For all for-profit properties, the top priority is to maintain the profitability of the investments. Therefore, finding new tenants and collecting rent are the top priorities of property managers. Most owners would prefer their property managers to submit operating statements on a monthly basis, including all necessary supporting documents such as a rent roll, arrears report, and expenses report.

Property managers should know how to perform preventive maintenance and routine maintenance using in-house maintenance staff or service contractors. Physical management and maintenance programs are covered in Chapter 5.

The operating budget, insurance coverage policy, and service contracts should also be prepared by the property managers and presented to the owners yearly together with the operating expenses report. Some owners prefer to have only annual reports; the monthly operating statements can be consolidated yearly.

When property managers have to manage a condominium complex, they will have to serve the board of directors to manage the whole building, not the individual unit owners. Although the property managers may have to deal with the individual units and their owners, the main task is to manage the building as a whole, especially the common areas of the complex.

Actually, the role of a condominium manager is to implement the decisions made by the board of directors and follow its instructions. Instead of renting out units and collecting rents, condominium property managers must promptly collect all monthly common element fees from the unit owners. There is no rent roll and arrears report, but they need to prepare status certificates (also known as estoppel certificates) for buyers or financial institutions upon request. The status certificate, prepared by the condominium manager and issued by the condominium corporation, is a document that sets out important details regarding the resale condominium unit and the condominium corporation. In some jurisdictions, condominium managers need to be licensed by passing specific courses and having a particular experience.

3. The Tenancy Agreement

Two of the duties of property managers are leasing out the building units and collecting rents from the tenant. During the leasing process, property managers must know how to screen prospective tenants. Once the tenants have moved in, property managers must know how to deal with the tenants in arrears. These two tasks are discussed in Chapter 4.

Although a tenancy agreement can be established orally in many jurisdictions, most landlords will work with the tenant to put it in writing to confirm the details. As professionals, property managers will ensure that a lease is signed before letting a tenant move in.

Tenancy Type

There are four types of tenancies: fixed-term tenancy, periodic tenancy, tenancy at will and tenancy at sufferance.

A fixed-term tenancy is a tenancy for a fixed length of time, which is generally agreed to in a written contract. In a fixed-term lease, both the commencement and expiry dates must be stated in the lease before the lease takes effect.

A periodic tenancy provides the tenant with exclusive possession for a fixed and repetitive period but indefinitely. The period can be yearly, monthly, weekly or else. The indefinite length can be made definite by notice of termination. Periodic tenancies are, usually, in writing.

A tenancy at will is a property tenure that either the landlord or the tenant may terminate at any time by giving reasonable notice. Unlike a periodic tenancy, it does not need any lease and usually does not specify the duration of the tenancy.

A tenancy at sufferance (also known as an overholding tenancy) exists when a person has possession without the consent of the landlord and until the landlord acts to evict the tenant from the property. A tenancy at sufferance usually occurs when the existing tenant refuses to vacate after a proper notice to quit or does not vacate after the fixed-term tenancy has expired.

In residential rental markets, the most common type of tenancies is periodic tenancies, and monthly tenancies are the norm. Tenancy at will should be avoided. In many jurisdictions, a fixed-term tenancy will become a month-to-month tenancy if it is not renewed. As a result, a tenancy at sufferance will not happen in that case.

Rent Type

There are three types of rent, gross rent, net rent, and percentage rent in commercial real estate leasing. There is another type of 'rent' – additional rent. However, it is not really rent, but the reimbursement of operating expenses from the tenants to the landlords. It is called a kind of 'rent' for legal purposes. Gross rent includes all operating expenses, except utilities. Net rent excludes all operating expenses which tenants have to pay. In residential, landlords charge only gross rent. Utilities may be included or excluded, depending on the landlords. What kind of utilities are included and excluded in the rent should be clearly stated in a lease.

One of the tasks of property managers is to reduce the operating expenses of the properties that they manage. Realty tax is one of the significant expenses of investment properties. The realty tax amount of a property is based on the value of that property. Therefore, appealing the realty tax of an over-appraised property becomes one of the tasks of property managers.

If the assessed value of a property can be reduced, its realty tax will also be reduced. That is why property managers have to have a basic knowledge of real estate appraising. In addition to the ability to establish the market rent, the knowledge can also help them tell if the property value is assessed reasonably or not.

Since the residential rent is gross, that means 'everything' is inclusive, including realty taxes. There are court cases that ruled that once residential landlords successfully reduce the property taxes, they have to reduce their tenants' rents by the same amount since the rent is gross. That is, since residential rent includes realty taxes, they are paid by the tenants instead of the landlords. Therefore, once the realty taxes are reduced, the tenants should take the benefit, not the landlords.

Although it costs the landlords to appeal the assessed values of their properties and not benefit from reducing realty taxes, the landlords still benefit from appealing the over-assessed value. The benefit is that when there is a vacancy, there is no tenant to pay the rent, which includes the real taxes. In other words, a low realty tax level can save landlords money when there is a vacancy. Moreover, the landlords can get a higher rent (or charge the original rent before reduction) when the existing tenants move out. Keeping the operating expenses at a low level is always a good idea for landlords.

Essential Components of a Lease

A lease is a rental agreement between a landlord and a tenant by which the landlord gives the tenant the right to use the leased premises for a period of time in exchange for the payment of rent. Unless the government requires all landlords to use its standard lease, landlords are free to draft their own lease agreements. Many lease formats have been developed over the years in different jurisdictions, reflecting increased sophistication and changes in such significant areas as tax law and common law. A sample tenancy agreement is illustrated in Appendix 2.

There are six essential components in a lease agreement, they are:

- Names of all parties
- Description of the leased premises
- Statement of consideration
- Legality of use
- Commencement and expiration dates
- Rules and Regulations

Names of All Parties

For property managers acting on behalf of the landlord, the name of the landlord can be the name of the property management company. Caution must be made if the property manager does not have a trust account for the landlord to deposit rental money since the tenants must make cheques payable to the landlord's name.

If the property management company uses its name as the landlord's name, all rents will be paid to the property management company, and it must have a trust account to hold the money for the landlord. If the property management company does not have a trust account for the landlord, it should not use its name as the landlord's name.

The names of tenants should include all adult residents in the rental units. Cosigners are, in fact, co-tenants and their names should be included in the name of tenants too.

Cosigners have the same right, obligations and liabilities as tenants.

If a guarantor or indemnitor is required for a particular tenant, the name of the guarantor or indemnitor should also be included in the lease. A guarantor is a person or legal entity that guarantees the rental payment of the tenant. If the money owing is not rent-related, the guarantor is not obligated to pay. An indemnitor has a higher liability and is liable for all damages caused by the tenant, including physical damages on the premises.

Description of the Leased Premises

The leased premises should be fully described in the lease, including a description of the rental building type, a single-family detached house, duplex, triplex, high-rise apartment or condominium complex, and the number of parking spots if there are any. Usually, the municipal mailing address is good enough to be used as the description. Sometimes, a site plan or a floor plan is used to prevent misunderstanding. For example, the parking site for a mobile home inside a mobile home site can be renumbered by the owner at any time. A site plan showing each parking spot with the rented spot highlighted is a better description than using the parking spot number.

Statement of Consideration

In contract law, consideration is a promise – the reason why a person should consider the contract. It should be a promise for a promise. A landlord gives the tenant the right to use the leased premises for a period of time in exchange for the payment of rent.

A lease must spell out how much money the tenant will pay, the payment frequency, the lease expiry date (subject to renewal) and the renewal terms and conditions (if applicable).

Legality of Use

Not all residential premises are designed for only residential use. There are mixed-use properties built, but the current structure supports only residential use. There are also residences built on lands with mixed-use zoning. Of course, the tenants may also illegally use the premises for non-residential use. Therefore, property managers must confirm with the tenants in the lease that the property can only be used as residential and nothing more.

Commencement and Expiration Dates

The commencement date of the tenancy should be the first day of a month. If the tenant wants to move in on another date, property managers should insist on using the first day of the following month to be the lease commencement date. They can charge prorated rent for the extra days before the first day of that month. Although it is legal and convenient to use the tenant's actual move-in date as the lease commencement date, it would be a nightmare for the property manager to collect rent.

Suppose a building has 100 units, and the tenants pay their rent on each date differently. In that case, the property manager would have to collect rent from three tenants every day on average. Usually, property managers will ask for a minimum lease term of one year to reduce the tenants' turnover rate.

<u>Rules and Regulations</u>

All rules and regulations should be disclosed to the tenant before they commit to a tenancy. Usually, they are a schedule attached to the lease, and they are printed separately for existing tenants to keep. Typical rules include no smoking, no waterbed, no business activities and no pet.

These essential components form the basic framework of a lease. Except for the Rules and Regulations, all other components will be changed according to the background and nature of the tenants.

Standard Clauses

Most of the leases, commercial and residential, are drafted by lawyers. Although lawyers are trained to be professionals in the legal field, not all of them are trained to specialize in real estate. Residential leases need to comply with the local tenancy law, and their main purpose is to protect the landlords. Property managers should have the basic knowledge of drafting a residential lease. At least, they should know what kinds of clauses are essential, and which clauses should be amended according to the background of each tenant, and which cannot be amended or deleted. Below are some standard clauses:

Payment

This clause should state the annual and monthly rent and when payment is due, and the payee's name. If the occupancy date is not the first day of a month, the rent should be prorated. The prorated rent should also be stated in this clause.

List of Occupants

A complete list of all occupants should be included in a lease. The list does not include the consigners who will not reside in the rental unit but includes children and infants. The primary purpose of this list is to make sure that the number of occupants will not exceed the maximum number of persons allowed by the municipal bylaws. For example, some municipalities may require the maximum number of persons living in a habitable unit not to exceed one person for every ten square metres of habitable unit floor area.

Deposit

This clause talks about the amount of deposit and prepaid rent, including how much the deposit and prepaid rent are. The clause should also tell when and how the deposit will be returned or credited to the tenant. There is a deposit limit in many jurisdictions that a landlord can charge the tenants and how the money should be returned.

Services and Facilities

This clause spells out the services, facilities and equipment available to the tenants and whether they are free to use or not. If they are not free, the fee structure should also be stated. The legal meaning of "free to use" is not the same as "included in the rent". Say a piece of equipment is out of order. If the use of that equipment is free to use, the landlord has no obligation to fix it or replace it. If the use of that equipment is included in the rent, the landlord must repair or replace it. Otherwise, the tenant can apply for a reduction of rent since the services or features included in the lease have been reduced.

Quiet Enjoyment

In common law, quiet enjoyment does not mean a state of quietness. The retail tenants do not want the mall to be quiet in a shopping mall, which means it has no shoppers. It means a landlord is required not to interfere or intrude upon the tenant's premises and let the tenants enjoy their space freely. In residential tenancies, it includes a certain level of noise control.

Under the covenant of quiet enjoyment, the landlord will not directly or indirectly interfere with or disrupt the tenant of the leased premises during the lease term. The freedom from noise, odour, pollution or disruption due to activities of other tenants is also part of quiet enjoyment.

Many residential leases do not have a clause to talk about quiet enjoyment as it is a landlord's covenant under the common law, which is implied and understood. However, most commercial leases will have a clause to restate such a landlord covenant.

Utilities

This clause spells out the utilities included in the lease, at the tenant's expense or optional. If a utility is to be paid by the tenant, the clause should state whether it is based on a flat fee or a separate metre.

Alterations and Additions

The clause deals with the alterations or additions of the unit. No such works should be done without the landlord's written consent, which may affect the overall structure, feature, or use of the building. Such alterations or additions may also affect compliance with local municipal, fire or building bylaws. Sometimes, the colour and style of window blinds are also regulated to maintain the whole building in the same style and outlook.

Repair and Maintenance

It is the landlords' responsibility to maintain the building, including the roof, structure and bearing walls.

Usually, the tenants will be responsible for all repairs to the interior of its premises and maintaining it in a sanitary condition. The responsibilities should be spelled out in this clause. If the landlord supplies the units with appliances or furniture, the repair and maintenance of those items should also be clearly stated in this clause.

Limitations of Landlord's Liability

This clause protects the landlords from the tenants' claims regarding damages caused by the landlord or happens on the premises. It disclaims the liabilities of the landlords for any personal injury or death that may be suffered or sustained by the tenants. It also states that the landlords are not liable for any loss of, damage or injury to any property, including cars and contents belonging to the tenant.

Indemnity of Landlord

This clause, also known as a "hold harmless" clause, requires the tenants to indemnify and save the landlord harmless with all claims for bodily injury or death, and property damage, except for damage covered by insurance. This clause will also ensure that the tenants acknowledge that they are responsible for any act or omission of an assignee or subtenant.

Insurance

This clause requires the tenant to maintain an insurance policy that provides comprehensive general public liability insurance for the leased premises for not less than a certain amount, usually $1,000,000 to $2,000,000 coverage or more. It also usually requires that the landlord be named one of the insured entities in the policy so that the landlord may file a claim directly to the insurance company. Another benefit of naming the landlord one of the insured entities is that the landlord will be notified by the insurance company whenever the tenants terminate, amend or fails to renew the policy.

Assignment and Subletting

A tenant may need to assign or sublet the rental unit for personal reasons, such as financial problems or relocation. In such cases, landlords will wish to exercise control of the assignment and subletting of their leases. In many jurisdictions, a tenant's right to assign or sublet is protected by law. That is, landlords may not be able to refuse such requests at their sole discretion. However, a standard clause requiring the tenants to get the landlord's written consent before assigning or subletting is still inserted into the lease to protect landlords better. It will be explained in the "Independent Clause" in the section "Special Clauses" below.

Abandonment and Right to Relet

Abandonment does not simply mean that the tenant has vacated the unit. Another condition that must be satisfied is that the tenant is in arrears of rent. A tenant can leave a unit vacant while paying rent and will not cause an abandonment. This clause provides the landlord with the power to retake possession of the rented premises and relet it out after an abandonment without the need for a court order terminating the tenancy. Such a right is subject to the local tenancy law and may need an "Independent Clause" to protect the legality of this clause.

Special Clauses

Not all leases are the same, but there are some clauses that property managers should ensure they are in the lease to protect the landlords better. Some governments require landlords to use the government standard form to sign the lease with tenants. In that case, landlords and property managers can insert the clauses into the form. The special clauses are:

Proof of Insurance

Although there is an insurance clause in most leases, many landlords did not check proof of insurance before handing out their keys. As a result, the tenant has no insurance to cover but gets possession. Since the tenant did not buy any insurance, the landlord will not be notified by the insurance company. Therefore, proof of insurance should be a prerequisite for the tenants to get their keys. A clause to request a copy of the insurance policy to show the policy is in place should be inserted into the lease, and it should be used as a condition for the tenant to get the keys.

Inspection Clause

The lease should have a clause to let the property manager inspect the premises to ensure that the maintenance work can be done promptly with proper notice in advance. In addition to the purpose of maintenance, another reason to insert such a clause into a lease is to prevent the tenant from performing illegal activities in the unit. Since the property manager has the right to inspect the unit at any time, if a prospective who intends to use the rental unit for illegal activities, he or she will be reluctant or refuse to rent the unit because of this clause.

No-pet Clause

This clause is used to disallow all kinds of pets on the premises. Service animals are not classed as pets, so they should be excepted. No-pet clauses are void in some jurisdictions under their tenancy laws, but they should still be inserted to protect the landlords when the law changes.

No-smoking Clause

More and more landlords want to make their building smoking-free. While it may be challenging to deal with existing smoker tenants, a non-smoking clause can ensure the new tenants will not smoke on the premises. Once all the existing smoker tenants move out, the building can be a smoking-free building. Note that a "no smoking" clause is not the same as a "no smokers" clause. A no-smoking clause disallows everyone to smoke on the premises, including visitors. A no-smoker clause means the tenants cannot be smokers, but the visitors can smoke on the premises. Moreover, a smoker can be a good tenant that obeys the rule by not smoking on the premises.

Independent Clause

In some jurisdictions, landlords and tenants cannot contract out of the law. If there is any clause in a lease that contradicts the law, the lease will be void even if both parties have agreed to it. For example, if the law says a landlord cannot disallow the tenant to have a pet, then a no-pet clause in a lease will not be valid even if both parties have agreed to it and signed the lease.

However, many leases still have a no-pet clause even though the law does not allow the landlord and tenant to contract out of the law. The reason is that the law may change sooner or later. The no-pet clause is illegal or unenforceable today does not mean that it will be illegal forever. Therefore, a professionally drafted lease will still have the clause to protect the landlords if the law changes in the future; the clause will become effective and enforceable once the new law allows the landlords to ban pets on their premises. Otherwise, the landlord will have to amend the leases, but the tenants can refuse to sign on the amended leases when the new law is passed

There is a risk of having an unenforceable or illegal clause in a lease. That single illegal clause may make the whole lease also become illegal and unenforceable. To avoid it, we need to add another clause such as the one below:

> *Should any provision or provisions of the lease be illegal or not enforceable, it shall be considered separate and savable from the lease. Its remaining provisions shall remain in force and be binding upon the parties hereto as thought the said provisions had never been included.*

With the clause above, the clauses currently illegal and unenforceable can stay in the lease without affecting the legality of the lease, but they will become legal and enforceable once the law is changed in that direction.

4. Administrative Procedures

Marketing the Building

Before a unit can be rented out, the property manager may have to advertise or promote the availability of units to attract prospective tenants. Promotions can also raise the image of the building in public, hence increase its value by charging a higher rent.

More and more property managers rely on online marketing tools and social media to promote their properties or getting referrals from existing tenants. Some rental buildings have their own bulletin boards to share the unit availability with their tenants. Some have the enquiry telephone number printed on their rooftop. Regardless of the marketing tools used, there are common steps for property managers to follow. They are:

- Market research and analysis
- Space planning
- Design of presentations
- Placement of advertisements
- Direct mailing
- Telephone follow-up
- Meetings with prospective tenants
- Building tours
- Lease negotiations

Market Research and Analysis

Property managers should know the rental trends, supply and demand, rental unit inventory, absorption rates, vacancy rates and the current rental rate in the neighbourhood.

An absorption rate is the number of units rented over a specific period, such as monthly, quarterly or yearly. Typically, property managers prefer net absorption rates as they include vacant units. A net absorption rate is the number of units rented less the number of units vacated during the period under analysis.

Property managers should also know their own buildings well, including the building's age, physical condition, special features, and necessary improvements. They should also be familiar with the demographic and geographic characteristics of the neighbourhood, the accessibility and proximity to amenities.

Space Planning

Based on market research, property managers should be able to decide what types of space will suit the prospective tenants most. Do the prospective tenants need parking spaces? Do they need lockers? Do they prefer smaller units over big units? The building space may be repartitioned with a minimal cost to best suit the tenants' needs.

<u>Design of Presentations</u>

Property management involves the presentation of the rental buildings to prospective tenants. The presentation methods include traditional printing such as brochures, letter mails, and signage; online tools such as social media and corporate websites. All of them involve graphic design as well as descriptive texts to attract people. Property managers have to ensure that all the descriptions, including room sizes, are correct.

<u>Placement of Advertisements</u>

There are many channels to place an advertisement. Some of them are free of charge, such as the free pages on social media or the exterior of the rental buildings. Some of them are fee-based, such as paid online ads or local newspapers and rental magazines. Property managers will place their ads on different channels, not just based on their budgets but according to their target markets and the market position of their buildings.

<u>Direct Mailing</u>

Depending on the characteristics of the buildings, some property managers will keep in touch with their previous tenants to promote their buildings and get referrals from the previous tenants. Newsletters are the most common type of materials used in direct mailing programs. The contents may include the recent upgrades of the buildings, the neighbourhood developments and the rental housing market trends. Direct mailing is more commonly used in some up-scale furnished apartments, and their targets are corporations that rent temporary housing units for their out-of-town executives.

Telephone Follow-up

Prospective tenants may inquire about all the rental buildings available in the neighbourhood and look for the best suits. Following up with the callers to offer more information and a building tour may increase the chance of renting out the units. When there is no vacancy in the building, property managers should keep the contact information of the callers and call them immediately whenever there is a vacant unit in the building; some of them may still be looking for a rental unit.

Meetings with Prospective Tenants

When there are prospective tenants, it is vital to meet them face-to-face to get a better understanding of them. The way they talk and behave may indicate how cooperative and honest they are. It is like a job interview to know the personalities of the applicants during the interview. Sometimes, property managers will allow their intuition to guide them.

Building Tours

There may be more than one unit that fits the prospective tenant's requirements. Property managers should show all the available units that fit their requirements to the prospective tenants. Showing the building to prospective tenants can also ensure that the building fits their requirements and expectations before they commit to renting a unit so that they may stay in the building for a longer time. It is also part of the 'orientation' that property managers organize to let their tenants get familiar with the building features, such as the laundry facilities.

<u>Lease Negotiations</u>

There is no guarantee that all leases negotiated will be accepted by the tenants or the property managers. Through the negotiation process, both property managers and prospective tenants can better understand the needs and expectations of the other party so that they can reduce the possibility of making wrong decisions.

Tenant Selection

Once the property managers get prospective tenants interested in renting their units, the next step is selecting the most suitable tenants from the responses.

Property managers can avoid many management problems that might arise due to tenants by selecting the best-qualified applicants. One of the issues to consider is to find tenants who are compatible with the building and who will remain there for extended periods of time. A more stable occupancy of a building can produce a more successful investment because of the low vacancy rate. It will also be less stressful for the property manager to manage a building with a low tenant turnover rate.

The criteria for the selection of the right tenants will differ from building to building. Some buildings fit seniors and retirees, while some buildings target big families with children. Property managers have the right to set their own tenant selection criteria as long as they are not discriminative under the human rights code or illegal under the relevant law. Typical criteria to select the most desirable residential tenants include that the tenant should:

- be able to pay the rent on time;
- not be noisy or disruptive;
- fit the building for long-term occupancy; and
- be cooperative and obey the rules and regulations of the building.

The process of tenant selection actually starts with the tenant application form. The tenant application form is used to collect information regarding the prospective tenant and assess the tenant's quality. A sample tenant application form is attached as Appendix 3. A photo ID, check of credit, employment letter and reference letter are usually required too.

Property managers can get rich information regarding the tenant from the tenant application form and the related documents. The most common photo ID is a driver's license. Property managers should know how to tell if a driver's license number is a fake one or not. Different states and provinces have their own method for assigning driver's license numbers, but the property managers should know the local method.

For example, the driver's license numbers in Ontario start with the first alphabet of the driver's last name and then a series of numbers. The last six digits will be the birth date of the driver in the format of YYMMDD. Therefore, Lesley Doe, whose birth date was Dec 22, 1999, would have a driver's license number Dxxxx-xxxx9-91222. If Lesley is a lady, then 50 will be added to the month digits, making the driver's license number Dxxxx-xxxx9-96222. Therefore, a property manager can rely on an Ontario driver's license number to tell the first letter of the last name, the gender and the birth date of that driver.

If the prospective tenant is currently renting and has filled in the previous landlord's information, the property manager should not waste time contacting the current landlord for a reference. It is because the comment from the current landlord will always be good. If the prospective tenant is good, the current landlord will say good. If the prospective tenant is not good, the current landlord will still say good to get rid of the tenant. A better approach is to contact the previous landlords as they are freer to tell without any conflict of interest.

The information of referees is essential. Property managers may contact them for references in addition to those from the landlords. Moreover, suppose the tenant abandons the unit and disappears. In that case, the property manager may contact the referees to get the latest contact information of the tenant to serve a claim or garnishment for the rent owed.

A credit report of the prospective tenant can be used to verify the information shown on the rental application form, such as the current and previous addresses, employers, date of birth and SIN. More importantly, property managers look for the overall credit rating and the credit history of the prospective tenant.

Different credit bureaus, such as TransUnion and Equifax, may have different scores for the same person, and the difference can vary by 100 points or more. Sometimes prospective tenants will pick the one that is more favourable to them to show it to the landlords. Therefore, the credit history of the prospective tenant plays a more important role here. If there are two or more R2 ratings (late payment of 30 days), the prospective tenant will not be considered desirable, and many landlords will refuse their applications.

Asking for an employment letter may be a convenient way to prove the prospective tenant's income level. However, there are cases that the letters are fake, the companies do not exist, or the prospective tenants or their spouse own the companies and write the letters for themselves. Property managers can search online for the company name, which may help them find helpful information regarding the company. Bank statements showing the salary payments or a tax return showing the annual net income is a better way to prove the income of a prospective tenant.

All the information and documents gathered during this stage are subject to the governance of privacy law. Property managers should have a system to comply with the requirements of the related rules and regulations. After this tenant selection process, all records should be saved and stored securely or destroyed according to the requirements of the law.

Moving In and Out

When a tenant moves out, the property manager should change the unit door lock core for safety reasons, unless the keys cannot be reproduced by the locksmiths and there is no loss in keys. Some locks have key-control functions that protect against unauthorized duplication of keys. The high-end ones can even deter unauthorized 3D printed copies of keys. Many condominiums and up-class rental buildings use that types of locks. Property managers should keep records of all the keys lost and change the lock core whenever a key is lost.

Changing the lock cores instead of changing the lock itself can ensure that all unit door locks will be compatible with the master key so that the property manager can open the doors in case of an emergency. Moreover, changing the lock core is less expensive and more manageable than changing the whole lock. Onsite staff, such as the superintendents, are capable of doing it with the proper tools and training.

The tenants and property manager should inspect all rental units before the tenants move in and move out. A sample inspection form is included in Appendix 4. Digital photos can be used to record the conditions of the unit, especially for damages.

If the building has elevators, the tenants will have to reserve one elevator for moving while other tenants can use the rest. Property managers have to schedule the booking of elevators and make sure that the tenants pay a security deposit for using the elevator. In case they cause any damage to the elevator, the security deposit will be used to repair the elevator.

If the lease commencement date is the first day of a month, then the tenant should only be allowed to move in on the first day of that month. Similarly, the tenant must move out by the last day of a month if the rent is paid on the first day of each month. However, if the lease commencement date is a Sunday or public holiday, the tenant may want to move in the day before, and some property managers are willing to accommodate that. Property managers must ensure that the tenants who are allowed to take possession before the lease commencement date will have their insurance policy effective when they get the keys, even if it is in the evening. A simple rule that property managers must follow is *No Insurance, No Key*. Unit inspection should also be done on or before the day they get the keys.

When delivering the keys, property managers should ask the tenants to acknowledge their receipt and agree to the costs for replacement or additional keys. A sample Tenant Receipt of Keys is inserted in Appendix 5. Some jurisdictions allow landlords to charge a key deposit. If the property managers want to charge such a security deposit, it should be stated in the lease so that the tenants will be well aware of that.

Serving Notices

Once the tenants have moved in, property managers will have to communicate with them for different purposes. There may be works to be done on the building that will affect the tenants, such as shutting off the water supply to service the pipes or tanks. There may be security issues that the management wants to alert the tenants about, such as car thieves or break-ins in the neighbourhood. The property managers, on and off, may also want to remind the tenants to follow their rules and regulations, such as not parking their cars in the reserved parking areas. These communications are usually done by posting a notice on the notice board, inside the elevators, at the main entrance door, or on the wall next to the elevator.

When an issue is related to a particular tenant, such as a failure to pay rent on time, the notice will not be posted and will be served directly to that tenant. Depending on the nature of the issue, many jurisdictions have rules for the landlords to follow when serving notices, such as non-payment, eviction and rent increase.

Some notices require 30 days for the notice to be effective; some require 60 days or 90 days. Correctly counting the days is crucial as it will affect the legality of a notice. If a notice is served incorrectly in common law, it is null and void and treated as it has never existed. For example, if a notice is served only 89 days in advance to increase the rent while the law requires at least 90 days in advance, such notice is invalid. The landlord cannot wait for one more day, not even one more month, to collect the increased rent. The notice is treated as if it does not exist, so the landlord cannot rely on the invalid notice to increase the rent by allowing more time for the service to be valid. A new notice must be served again to comply with the law.

People always make one common mistake: they count the number of days but failed to understand that a 30-days notice actually means it needs one calendar month as the notifying period. A 60-day notice needs two calendar months, and a 90-days notice needs three months.

Suppose a tenant starts a tenancy on the first day of December. After one year, the tenant wants to end the tenancy and sends the landlord a notice to terminate it. If the law requires a 60-day notice before a tenancy can be terminated and the tenant wants to move out by the end of November, then the tenant must send the notice on or before October 1st.

Similarly, if the tenant wants to move out by the end of August, a notice must be sent on or before July 1st. Many people thought there are 31 days in both July and August (62 days in total), so they can serve the 60-day notice on or before July 3rd (29 days remaining in July). Together with the 31 days in August, they thought it fulfills the 60-day requirement. That is a wrong counting method. When we count the 30 days after a notice is given, we do not count by days but by months. A 60-day notice needs two whole months. If the notice is given after July 1st, then the month of July is not counted as a whole month, so the notice is only a 30-days notice; hence it is not valid.

There are only 28 days in the month of February, except in a leap year. Therefore, there is a special rule for counting the days in January, February and March. The rule allows notices to be sent by giving less than 60 days when they are served by counting in February. Say, if the end of February is the last day of a tenancy, the termination notice can be given no later than January 1st. If the tenant is moving out at the end of March, the 60-day notice can be given no later than February 1st.

Money Matters

Property managers collect rent and pay the expenses for the owners. Therefore, property management companies should have a trust account for each owner and each building to separate the money from their own and distinguish the funds among different owners and buildings. The trust account designated for a particular building will only be used to deposit the rent and other income collected from that building and pay expenses related to the operation of that building.

Some jurisdictions require landlords to pay interest on the deposits they get from their tenants. The interest rate usually is either a rate fixed by the government or floating according to an index, usually the Consumer Price Index. Property managers will pay the interest for the owners from the trust account. On the other hand, they will also put the money collected from rental payments into an interest-bearing account to get some interest for the owners. It is rare, although possible that there is a clause in the lease to require the landlords to pay interest on the deposit they are holding if it is not required by law.

Most property managers will require the tenants to pay one month's rent in advance and one month's rent as a deposit for the last month's rent when they sign a lease with the prospective tenants. The last month's rent should be "topped up" whenever there is a rent increase. The tenant should pay the increased amount to the deposit as the last month's rent has been increased.

For example, a tenant moved into a unit and paid $1,000 as the deposit for the last month's rent. The property manager increased the rent to $1,050 after a year. The property manager should have asked the tenant to pay $50 to top-up the deposit. Otherwise, the deposit held by the property manager would remain $1,000, which is less than one month's rent (the last month's rent).

Property managers should issue rent receipts to tenants each month. Some of them select to issue the receipts on a yearly basis which saves labour and costs. However, monthly rent receipts are better proof of payments whenever there is an argument in rent paid or late payments. It may help the rental tribunals save time in judging non-payment cases if monthly rent receipts are used and issued as a common practice by property managers.

It is expected that some tenants would not pay their rent on time every month. Some of them may have financial difficulties, and some may just forget to do so. For those who have financial problems, it may turn out that the property managers have to serve formal notice to request payment and may eventually have to apply for an eviction order to have the tenants moved out.

When a tenant fails to pay rent on the due day, a Default Notice should be served immediately after that day. Depending on the jurisdictions, some landlords must serve a Notice to End a Tenancy Early because of the non-payment of rent instead of a default notice. A default notice is used to notify the tenants that they have not paid the rent as stipulated in the lease so that the landlord may take necessary actions accordingly. A notice to end a tenancy early for the non-payment of rent is the first step that landlords must do in those jurisdictions before applying to the tribunals to terminate a tenancy.

If a property manager fails to serve such notice immediately after the rent due date, it will delay the process of evicting the tenant afterwards. On the other hand, if the tenant pays the rent within a specific time upon receiving the notice (usually two weeks), the notice to end a tenancy early will be void automatically.

In some jurisdictions, agency property management companies cannot represent the owners in front of the rental tribunals unless they are named the landlord in the lease. They may even not be allowed to serve notices on behalf of the owners. Such notice will be null and void if they do, and the tribunal will dismiss the case.

The rationale behind this is that property management companies are not law firms, and they are not supposed to provide any legal services to their clients. Legal services include the drafting of notices, applications and the serving of notices; and are not limited only to representing the owners on the day of the hearing in front of the tribunal.

In some jurisdictions, property managers must be licensed and, as a result, they may represent the owners in front of the rental tribunals.

5. Physical and Operational Management

One of the duties of property managers is to maintain the buildings that they manage. Not only are property managers involved in the maintenance process, site managers, other on-site staff and property owners, are also involved in the process by giving the judgement of the physical appearance of the properties and works to be done. The lack of maintenance of the buildings will seriously affect the rental income of the properties. Poor building conditions may increase the insurance premiums, which also affects the owners' ability to refinance the properties.

Buildings and other improvements on the lands are subject to deterioration either from age or lack of care. Therefore, there will always be repairs necessary due to ageing, normal wear and tear, malfunctions, breakages or vandalism. Works as simple as keeping the properties clean and tidy may prevent or low down repair needs. The building maintenance that property managers have to organize can be grouped into the following categories:

- Routine maintenance to keep the premises clean and tidy, such as maintaining the landscaping, clearing snow and ice, disposing of garbage
- Preventive maintenance to prevent deterioration, such as applying waterproof material to wood structures, replacing aged components

- Corrective maintenance to repair wear and tear, breakages, and damages caused by vandalism, such as replacing shingles, repairing broken equipment, cleaning graffitis

Property managers or on-site superintendents should inspect the exterior and interior of the buildings regularly and maintain a logbook for the inspections. A sample maintenance checklist is included in Appendix 6.

Routine Maintenance

Routine maintenance usually relates to the common areas and facilities shared by the occupants, such as the parking lot, elevators, stairs, concourse and corridor. The inspection and maintenance are usually performed by a combination of maintenance and janitorial staff, who are also responsible for a broad range of daily tasks, including but not limited to:

- Floor cleaning and polishing
- Light bulbs replacement
- Entrance door cleaning
- Refuse and recycling material pickup
- Ventilation filter cleaning or replacement
- Landscape maintenance
- Parking lot and walkway sweeping
- Snow and ice removal
- Elevator inspection and cleaning

- Smoke alarms and CO detectors testing
- Fire alarm testing
- Fireplace chimney cleaning

Floor Cleaning and Polishing

A well-polished floor represents that the building is well-maintained and managed. Besides presenting the building with a clean and neat image, cleaning the floor is essential for safety measures. A slippery floor is dangerous, especially for seniors. Floor cleaning includes cleaning the rugs and runner carpets at the entrance, concourse, corridors and inside the elevators.

Light Bulbs Replacement

A well-lited environment can increase safety, especially at night and indoor. Not only the property managers but all onsite and visiting staff should also pay attention to the lights throughout the common area and notify the property managers to replace light bulbs, broken or inoperative fixtures as required.

Entrance Door Cleaning

The appearance of the main entrance gives the visitors and prospective tenants the first impression of the quality of the building and the management. All glass at entrances should be cleaned and washed regularly to maintain its cleanliness and clarity, which is also essential for security monitoring purposes.

Refuse and Recycling Material Pickup

Each rental building should apply strict regulations and implicit instructions for the disposal of garbage and recycling materials. Garbage and recycling materials are usually collected under contract by a waste management company utilizing various containers located in the service area of the building. Tenants are required to drop their garbage and recycling materials in their respective containers. There should be operations hours for dropping the garage or recycling material, especially if it is a high-rise building using garbage chute systems,

Ventilation Filter Cleaning or Replacement

Most rental buildings use central heating systems with individual thermostats and filters in the units. Although it is the tenant's responsibility to maintain the heating and ventilation units inside their homes, many property management companies provide filter cleaning or replacement services to them free of charge.

Landscape Maintenance

Beautiful landscaping can improve the overall living environment of the rental complex, hence attracting prospective tenants and retaining existing tenants. Onsite staff can quickly notice debris, litter, and spills on the common outside areas with a well-shaped landscape. Lawns, trees and flowers should be fertilized at least once a year or according to their needs.

Parking Lot and Walkway Sweeping

Parking lots and walkways should be clear of litter and debris. In particular, all pedestrian crossing in the parking lots, interior and exterior walkways, passenger pickup and dropoff areas at the entrance or near the garage should also be free from obstacles and spills.

Snow and Ice Removal

Depending on the locations, property managers may have to arrange snow and ice removal services by contracting the services to outside contractors or hiring onsite or head office maintenance crews. For removing the snow in the parking lots, clear instructions must be given to the snow shovelers to pile the snow on the extreme peripheral area of the parking lot and avoid covering the catch basins and fire hydrants.

After the thaw, it is crucial to have the catch basins cleaned out as there will be accumulations of debris and leaves that may block the storm drains and possibly cause flooding of the parking lot or sidewalks.

Elevator Inspection and Cleaning

Many emergency calls from high-rise buildings are related to elevators, especially from old buildings. Onsite staff should be trained to talk to the people trapped inside, calm them down and seek assistance as quickly as possible. The best solution to it is to avoid elevator malfunctions by regularly inspecting the elevators. The elevator cabs should also be cleaned regularly to maintain their cleanliness to avoid any debris falling into the elevator slots, which may cause elevator malfunctions.

Smoke Alarm and CO Detectors Testing

Smoke alarms and carbon monoxide detectors, including those in the common areas and inside rental units, should be tested at least twice a year. If the detectors are battery-operated, property managers should make sure the batteries are replaced every year or according to the user's guide.

Fire Alarm Testing

Besides smoke alarms, central fire alarm systems are usually installed in rental buildings. Property managers should test the system at least once a year together with the PA system (if available). A fire drill should also be conducted at least once a year.

Fireplace Chimney Cleaning

If the building has fireplaces, the chimneys must be inspected and cleaned every year. All chimneys inside the units should also be inspected and cleaned. Soot, blockages and built-up creosote should be removed from the chimney liner, firebox, smoke chamber and damper.

Preventive Maintenance

Preventive maintenance is designed to keep building systems operating at peak efficiency. It is a planned and controlled program of improvements, adjustments, repairs and performance analysis. It focuses on the deficiencies in building systems and corrects them before they become problematic. A preventive maintenance program should be prepared and directed by the property manager of the building and carried out either using in-house building staff or through specialist contractors, at specific intervals or within certain time frames.

Structural Maintenance

Property managers must regularly inspect their buildings thoroughly to ensure that the buildings can be improved to save costs or have repairs on time to avoid structural damages. Different buildings need different types of maintenance, depending upon their ages, construction methods, types of finishes, and other factors. The frequencies of maintenance works and inspections also vary for each item. For example, exterior painting and caulking may be inspected every year, and interior painting and floorings may be inspected every three years or longer.

Property managers must first list the items that need preventive maintenance to set up a preventive structural maintenance program. Below are some of the typical items that might be included in a preventive structural maintenance program.

Exterior
- Check asphalt surface and fix
- Check caulking around windows and repair
- Check concrete surface and repair
- Check door locks and hinges, and repair
- Check exterior painting for repaint
- Check foundation and exterior walls for repair
- Check gutter and downspouts, and clean
- Check interlock brick sidewalks, and fix
- Check lighting and signs, and clean
- Check plants for viruses and insects, and fix
- Check sewer system and clean
- Check shingles and fix
- Check trees for power line interference

Interior
- Check door locks and hinges, and repair
- Check emergency exits and stairways
- Check exterior painting for repaint
- Check for damp spots to repair
- Check lobbies for an update
- Check the expiration date on the fire extinguisher
- Check washrooms for necessary update
- Check water pipes for leakage

After listing out the items to be included in the structural preventive maintenance program, the next step is to develop a schedule for each item. The entire program can be developed based on that schedule. The frequency of inspection can be frequent, short-term or long-term. Frequent means every year or every month, short-term means two or three years, and long-term is five to ten years. The following table shows how that could be done using the items listed above.

Frequent
- Asphalt Surface (when old)
- Concrete Surface (when old)
- Emergency Exits and Stairways
- Damp Spots
- Foundation and Exterior Walls
- Gutter and Downspouts
- Interlock Brick Sidewalks (when old)
- Lighting and Signs
- Plants
- Sewer System
- Shingles (when old)
- Water pipes

Short-term
- Caulking Around Windows
- Door Locks and Hinges
- Concrete Surface (when old)
- Washrooms

- Fire Extinguisher

Long-term
- Asphalt Surface (when new)
- Lobbies
- Concrete Surface (when new)
- Exterior Painting
- Interlock Brick Sidewalks (when new)
- Shingles (when new)

Once the schedules for the items have been assigned, a checklist with a calendar can be prepared for the onsite staff to perform the inspection and maintenance at the appropriate time.

Mechanical Maintenance

Depending on the building size and type, the complexity of the mechanical equipment varies among rental buildings. For example, a high-rise and luxury rental apartment will have elevators, water softeners, sprinkler systems, automatic doors and remote-controlled garage doors. A townhouse-style basic rental complex may not have any of them.

Due to the moving components, mechanical equipment demands more frequent and detailed maintenance than the structural items of a building. Regular inspections and maintenance can prevent breakdown or malfunctioning of the equipment, which are especially important for vital systems such as heating systems, elevators and water heaters.

Because of the high frequency of inspections and the complexity of the equipment, the preventive mechanical maintenance program requires various checklists and logbooks to maintain control and ensure that inspection procedures are being followed. Below are some of the typical items that might be included in a preventive mechanical maintenance program.

Electrical
- Aquastats
- Breaker panels
- Controls and gauges
- Lighting systems
- Emergency lighting
- Energy conservation system
- Thermostats
- Transformers

Fire Safety
- Alarm bells
- Alarm pull stations
- Annunciator panels
- Carbon monoxide (CO) detectors
- Heat detectors
- Smoke detectors
- Sprinkler systems

Heating and Cooling Systems

- Boilers
- Circulating pumps
- Compressors
- Cooling towers
- Fans
- Heat exchangers
- Sump pumps
- Vacuum pumps
- Water chillers
- Water heaters

Mechanical

- Automatic Disabled Doors
- Elevators
- Emergency generators
- Garbage compactors
- Garage Door Spring and Sensor
- Windows

Security and Surveillance

- CCTV cameras
- CCTV monitors
- Entry control systems
- Intercom systems
- Motion detectors
- Emergency help buttons

Some items in a preventive mechanical maintenance program may have to be inspected as frequently as every day. When the equipment has a manufacturer's operating manual, it must be inspected as specified in the operating manual. All onsite staff and contract service personnel who perform the inspections or repairs should be well-qualified, certified or licensed as per the requirements. They should also be required to sign in before performing any maintenance work and sign out before leaving, recording arrival time and departure time. The number of hours spent on the task can be checked against the quantity and complexity of the works done. It can also be used to check against the invoice of the contractor to ensure that the time spent meets contract requirements.

Corrective Maintenance

Despite effective routine and preventive maintenance procedures, buildings and other improvements are still inevitably subjected to various forms of breakage, failure or damage. Remedial measures must be taken immediately to avoid any discomfort, disturbance or inconvenience to the tenants, which can also prevent further damages to the building and maintain a good image of the building. Typical items that need immediate repairs include:

- Blocked sewers or drains
- Broken CCTV camera or monitor

- Broken fan belts
- Broken or cracked glass doors
- Broken washroom fixtures
- Broken windows
- Burned-out ballast
- Electrical overloads
- Frozen water lines
- Malfunction of an elevator
- Malfunction of entrance doors
- Malfunction of heating systems
- Malfunction of water heater
- Toilet overflow

Because of the emergency nature, the onsite staff is the best resource for minor correctional repairs such as blocked sewers and toilet overflow. Property managers must ensure that onsite staff will immediately respond to reports or complaints of any malfunction or damage.

If the problems are related to water from heavy rain, or damages caused by heavy winds, snow or ice pellets, the more quickly that repair is taken, the more minor the damage to the building and persons will be. Therefore, efficient communications are crucial to providing responsive actions. All maintenance and security staff should be equipped with a wireless communications system, such as walkie-talkies, cellphones and apps.

Minimizing Operating Expenses

One of the objectives of the maintenance programs is to prevent the building and other improvements from deteriorating, prolong their life and eventually lower the operating expenses of the building. That coincides with the primary objective of property management to obtain maximum revenue from a property at minimum expense. Minimizing the costs spent on maintenance programs without sacrificing the quality and safety of the building can be done through a few aspects.

Tenant Involvement

The tenants live in the building, use the building facilities on and off, and go through the common areas such as the main entrance and parking lot daily. They know the building better than the property managers. Property managers should encourage the tenants to report any damage they see immediately so that the repair works can be done in time.

To reduce the possibility of careless damages to the building and facilities, property managers should remind the tenants to abide by the building regulations. Typical rules include those relative to garbage disposal and the use and limitations of electrical appliances and equipment, especially the high-wattage ones.

Other rules that may help reduce maintenance and operating expenses include asking the tenants to keep the sewage systems unplugged by not dumping solid waste materials, including paper towels and feminine products, into the toilets. Tenants are also advised not to leave windows open to burden the air conditioning or heating systems. Those rules also apply to homeowners who want to save costs on their maintenance and utility bills. If all the tenants observed those rules and cooperate with the management, there could be savings in utility costs, plumbers' service costs, electricians' service costs and more.

Onsite Staff

Properties with onsite staff may perform better in saving maintenance costs and operating expenses. Onsite staff should be trained to have general knowledge in building maintenance, especially they must know when to report the damages to a higher level. They should also be fully informed about the role they play in building management. Depending on their skills, some of them can fix minor damages on the buildings; some can only escalate them to the management level. Either way, they can make sure the necessary work can be done as soon as possible.

When there is onsite staff in the buildings, the property managers should provide the proper tools for them to do routine building maintenance. The user's manual of the tools should also be provided to proper control and maintain all mechanical equipment, such as vacuum cleaners, polishers, mowers, snowblowers and parking lot sweepers. The onsite staff should have emergency telephone numbers handy, usually stored in their electronic devices, including service contractors, local police stations, fire stations, utility companies and local authorities such as public works.

The property managers should develop an operations manual for each building that outlines the procedures to be followed and the documentation to be used for different maintenance programs. The onsite staff should be provided with building plans that clearly show the locations of all shut-off valves for fire hose connectors, fire extinguishers, gas, and electrical breaker panels. The locations of the main water switch, sprinkler systems, and sump pumps and their controls should also be indicated on the plans. Most importantly, the onsite staff should be familiar with all life safety procedures and systems, including the situations of robberies and terrorist attacks.

Deferred Maintenance

Some landlords and property managers use deferred maintenance plans to keep their operating expenses at a minimum level, but the results are often the opposite. Deferred maintenance plans mean that they will delay some if not all, maintenance works to the later possible time. They believe that even if the same money must be used in maintenance, they can save the money according to the Time Value of Money – future money has a lower value. Therefore, they will perform the jobs as late as possible.

We cannot ignore the problems that have already occurred. If we do not perform the repair works immediately, the damages will worsen, and the costs of remedial works will far exceed the original costs. If there are not enough funds to do the works, the landlord should consider borrowing money to do them. Some landlords will defer their maintenance plan when they consider selling the building and pass the onus of repairs on to the new owner. However, a prudent buyer will take that into consideration; hence a lower purchase price will be offered to reflect such delayed maintenance.

Reporting

A series of forms should be used by property managers to monitor and report the maintenance programs in the buildings. A report on damage or deficiency should be used to tell the type of equipment, the degree of damage, and its location. The report should tell if special skills, usually mean only licensed technicians can perform the work, are required or not. For severe damages that involve a large amount of repair capital, the form will initiate the process of selecting contractors, such as the request for proposals.

Once a maintenance program is initiated, the property manager should use a daily maintenance report to keep track of the repairs being performed. The report can be used to assure the work will be done according to the schedule stated in the service contract, within the budget set in the operating budget and hence used as cost control.

6. Property Management Accounting

The main objective of real estate investments is to get stable cash flows through the collection of rents. To measure the profitability of an income-producing property, one has to know the amount of income generated and returned to the owner. The primary duty of property managers is to maximize the net operating income (NOI) generated by the rental properties under their management. That is why the management fees are often tied with the net incomes of the buildings.

Cash Flow Analysis

Property managers need to understand the cash flow calculation elements to attain the highest possible net operating income level with the lowest possible expenses. The higher the net operating income, the better performance of a property and its manager. Although not every factor contributing to NOI can be controlled, increasing rent, making extra income, reducing vacancy and bad debts, and controlling expenses will help maximize the NOI of a building.

Property managers may have to do a cash flow analysis to project the cash flows for a few years for different purposes. The most common reason is for the landlord to apply for a mortgage. The procedures for calculating the cash flow of a residential rental building can be found from the excerpt of the Cash Flow Analysis Worksheet below:

Ownership Analysis of Property Income   **Taxable Income**

		Year 1	Year 2
3	Potential Rental Income		
4	Minus: Vacancy & Credit Losses:		
5	Equals: Effective Rental Income		
6	Plus: Other Income		
7	Equals: Gross Operating Income		
8	Minus: Operating Expenses		
9	**Equals: Net Operating Income**		
10	Minus: Non-operating Expense		
11	Minus: Interest - 1st Mortgage		
12	Minus: Interest - 2nd Mortgage		
13	Minus: Amortization of Loan Fees		
14	Minus: Others		
15	Minus: Others		
16	Equals: Subtotal Taxable Income Before Depreciation		
17	Minus: Allowable Depreciation		
18	Equals: Real Estate Taxable Income		
19	Times: Marginal Tax Rate		
20	Equals: Tax Liability on Real Estate Operations		

Cash Flows

21	Net Operating Income		
22	Minus: Annual Debt Service		
23	Equals: Cash Flow Before Taxes		
24	Minus: Tax Liability (Line 20)		
25	**Equals: Cash Flows After Tax**		

Potential rental income is the maximum amount of income that a property can produce in one year. It is based on the assumption that all the units are fully occupied within the building at the highest possible legal rental rates. To maximize the potential rental income, property managers should know the rental market well so that they can charge the highest possible rent whenever there is a vacancy. The first step is to deduct the vacancy and credit losses from it with the potential rental income. The difference is called the effective rental income.

The vacancy and credit losses are usually a percentage of the potential rental income. A typical rate is between three to five percent, depending on the location, the number of units and leasing history of the building. The vacancy and credit losses can never be zero even though the building has had no vacancy rate for years because there is no guarantee that all tenants will pay their rent.

Most vacancies are caused by the moving out of the existing tenants, while some are caused by default in rental payments. Therefore, property managers must start looking for new tenants as soon as they receive notices from tenants to terminate their leases to reduce the vacancy period. A good tenant selection process can reduce the possibility of default in rental payments.

Other income, such as parking and laundry, is added to the effective rental income to produce the effective gross income. All expenses related to the operation of the rental income will be deducted from the effective gross income to produce the net operating income. The property management fee is part of the operating expenses.

Net operating income is the most direct way to measure a property manager's success. All property managers should try their best to attain the highest possible level of income and the lowest possible level of expenses without sacrificing maintaining the physical conditions of the property.

Usually, the task of property managers in cash flow analysis ends with the production of NOI. The landlords or their accountants will determine the cash flow before tax and after tax.

Trust Account

There are three types of property managers – agency management, in-house management and self-management. For agency management, the management companies are the agents of the landlords. They owe the landlords all the fiduciary duties under agency law, and one of the duties is accounting.

Simply speaking, accounting means the property manager should not mix their assets with the landlords' assets. Therefore, a property management company should have trust accounts to hold the money for different landlords. Even for the same landlord, if the landlord has different properties managed by the same property manager, the property manager should open different accounts for different properties for distinguishment. Similarly, for in-house management and self-management, the owners should also have separate accounts for different buildings to measure the performance of each building.

A trust account in property management is a bank account in the property management company's name, but the money is held in trust for the landlord of a rental building. The property managers or their supervisors will be the signing authorities. Usually, two signatures are required to ensure that the money will only be disbursed as required. The beneficiary is the landlord. All the interest earned by the money in the account also belongs to the landlord. The money is separated from the assets of the property management company. A trust account can protect a landlord's money from creditors' claims when the property management company goes bankrupt. All money that goes into and pays out from the trust account must be recorded in a trust account ledger.

Trust Account Ledger

It used to be an account book, but now it is a spreadsheet or software. The information in a trust account ledger should include the date, description of the entry, unit number, deposit amount, deposit reference, payment amount, issued cheque number, explanation and balance. The deposit and payment dates recorded in the ledger may not match the dates shown on the bank statements, the same for the balance. Therefore, reconciliations must be done each month to make sure there is no mistake.

Reconciliation involves comparing and matching figures from the trust account ledger to those shown on the bank statement. When the comparison is made, any transactions not found on the bank statement (or vice-versa) are said to be outstanding. The underlying purpose is to provide assurances that the transactions recorded by the bank and the actual operations of the trust account are in agreement concerning money on deposit.

A bank statement total may vary from the balance of the trust account ledger due to deposits that have been recorded but have not been confirmed by the bank and the issued cheques that have been recorded but not cashed. Reconciliation is necessary because the bank and the property management company are maintaining independent records of bank account activity, and differences must be reconciled. All reconciliations should be signed and dated by the property manager.

Reconciliation statements are prepared for the whole period of each month. Usually, a property manager will start preparing the reconciliation of the previous month upon receiving the bank statement. Any deposits received and cheques issued after the month-end will be dealt with in the reconciliation next month. The reconciliation does not need to detail all of the activity that occurs on the statement. The property manager does not need to list every deposit and every cheque on the reconciliation. The purpose of reconciliations is to confirm that the balances of the bank statements and the trust account ledger are the same or explain the discrepancies between the balance of the bank statements and the trust account ledger.

Accounting for Revenues

The revenues from rental buildings can be generated from several sources, including rent, parking, laundry, vending machines or other services. Property managers must keep the related documents for the audit trail and account for those revenues.

All leases should be stored as records. They indicate the original rent amounts, commencement dates and other relevant information about the tenancies. In many jurisdictions, residential rent increases are subject to rent control, and landlords must serve notices in advance for any rent increase. The original leases can be used to tell if the increased rents exceed the allowed percentage or not. The commencement date can tell if the notices are served with compliance or not. These are the essential documents for the buyer when the building is for sale in the future.

Property managers should keep a registry of the deposits paid by the tenants with duplicate receipt slips. Each of them must be identified by the unit number and the tenant's name. The registry should be cross-referenced to the tenant's ledger.

A tenant's ledger records the monthly rent received from each tenant each month, with their name and unit number. The ledger also provides a summary of tenants in arrears and those who are current with rents. The amount of deposit paid and the payment date should also be included in this ledger.

Accounting for Expenses

Property managers have to pay the bills for the landlords and must keep the bills. Disbursements include purchase orders, utility and tax bills, cash payments, management fees, tenant's refund and interest.

Purchase orders include the purchase of cleaning suppliers, contracted janitorial services and maintenance works done on the properties. Utility bills, including related services such as maintenance plans purchased from utility companies, should be kept for reference. Tax bills and property assessment notices should be filed together for easy reference. It will be helpful when the landlord wants to appeal the assessed value to reduce the property tax.

Sometimes property managers need petty cash to pay for small items or emergencies, such as no light bulb inventory in the management office. Receipts should be kept and filed with reference to the type of expenses. Cheques issued should also be recorded in the trust account ledger with cheque numbers, the date, the amount and the payee name.

Property managers may take out money from the trust account to pay for their management fees and other related expenses as agreed in their management contracts. All such reimbursements should be recorded in the trust account ledger with explanations. All interests paid and security deposits refunded to the tenants must be recorded with the unit number, date and the payee's name.

Reserve Fund

Every building needs repairs and preventive work to maintain its physical condition. Some maintenance works are expensive, so some landlords may have a cash flow problem if the maintenance plan is not well prepared in advance. Therefore, most jurisdictions require condominium buildings to have a reserve fund for major repair and replacement of building components and facilities such as roofs, building exterior finishes, common roads, sidewalks, heating systems, plumbing systems, recreational and parking facilities.

Although it is not required by law, many property management companies will set up reserve funds for their landlords to ensure they have sufficient money to perform all major repair works or replacements in the future. A small amount of money is saved into an interest-bearing account every month for different kinds of work to be done. After the estimated time, the principal and interest earned will be good enough for the repair works.

Setting up reserve funds, including the calculations of money to be saved in the reserve funds each month, becomes one of the most critical tasks for property managers.

Different types of work may have different time schedules and require different amounts of money. The total money required to be saved will be calculated using the concept of the Time Value of Money.

Time Value of Money

In the concept of the time value of money, the money we now receive (the present value) is worth more than the same amount in the future (the future value) because of the potential earning capacity if the money is invested today. Moreover, inflation makes the buying power of the same amount of money decrease over time.

In time value of money calculations, we will have to deal with the following numbers:

1. The Number of Periods in one year (P/YR)
2. The Present Value (PV)
3. The Interest Rate (I)
4. The Total Number of Periods for compounding (N)
5. The Periodic Payments within the period (PMT)
6. The Future Value (FV)

We need to know five of the above numbers to find the sixth one using a financial calculator or an app. The time value of money is a necessary consideration for investments. Its calculations involve the Six Functions of a Dollar. The six functions are:

1. Future Value

2. Present Value

3. Future Value of an Annuity

4. Present Value of an Annuity

5. Amortization of Future Value

6. Amortization of Present Value

In property management, we will deal with the Amortization of Future Value. Suppose a building needs an amount of money (FV) to replace its roof after a number of periods (N). Currently, there is no reserve fund for the replacement (PV = 0), and money is being contributed periodically, and it earns an interest rate (I) per period (P/YR = number of periods per year). We look for the money to be contributed in each period (PMT).

Property managers use spreadsheets or software to calculate the money required to save into a reserve fund each month. At the same time, financial calculators and apps are good for students to do simple tasks and exercises. There are free online apps[1] for easier operations than using financial calculators.

Example

Question

A property manager just accepted a contract to manage a rental apartment building. The roof of the building has just been replaced, and the property manager believes

---

[1] Such as https://www.fncalculator.com/financialcalculator?type=tvmCalculator

that the roof and other major components will have to be replaced again 30 years later. The estimated costs of the replacements are $3,000,000, valued 30 years later. The manager will set up a Pre-authorized Purchase Plan to buy a mutual fund that produces a minimum of 3% return per annum based on its history for the purpose of replacing the roof. Assuming that the mutual fund produces a 3% return per annum, calculated monthly, how much money will the property manager have to invest into the fund mutual fund each month?

Solution

The financial calculator should be set in the "Begin" mode if the money is invested on the first day of each month. It should be set in the "End" mode if the money is invested on the last day of each month. With the background information, we have:

P/YR = 12 (payments are made each month)

N = 360 (months)

PV = 0

I = 3%

FV = $3,000,000

and we look for the value of PMT

The PMT is –$5,135.28 (it is a negative value as the owners pay it out). It is based on a "Begin" mode. That is, the property manager has to set up a mutual fund account to buy the fund on the first day of each month.

Reporting

Property managers will usually send monthly financial activity reports, including information regarding income, expenses and cash flow to landlords. Other reports, including rent rolls, vacancy reports, delinquency reports and budget variance reports, will be sent annually.

A rent roll is a document that lists all the rentals in the property; usually, it has the unit numbers, corresponding tenant's name, lease commencement date, expiry date (or indicated as month-to-month), rent amount and other details.

A vacancy report lists the units that have been vacant during the reporting year and the duration of the vacancies. A delinquency report lists the name of the tenants who are in default, whether they have moved out or not, and the rent they owed. It also tells whether legal proceedings have started or a collecting agency is used.

A budget is a financial plan for a defined period of time, often one year, based on estimates of revenues and expenditures during that period. Property managers will prepare two types of budgets for the landlords – an operating budget that provides a standard against which to measure operating income and expenses; and a capital budget, which provides a standard against which to measure costs of major renovations or repairs.

Operating Budget

An operating budget is an itemized estimate of revenue generated by the rental property and the expenditure to operate the property. An operating budget focuses on the annual operating expenditures and will not contain capital expenditures and long-term loans.

Property managers will monitor actual revenue or expense against each budgeted item on a month-to-month basis. If there is a significant disparity, they may have to investigate the reasons or causes and take remedial actions if necessary. However, sometimes decrease in revenue and over-expenditures are unavoidable.

For example, many tenants lost their jobs during the pandemic period and could not pay rent. Some governments refused the landlords' applications for terminating the tenancies because of non-payment of rent until the situation was improved. If there is a hefty snowfall and it lasts for a few days, it will require additional snow-clearing services, and the cost may exceed the budget, which is based on an average annual snowfall. In those situations, no remedial action is required as the cause of the reduction in revenue and over-expenditure is beyond everyone's control.

If a property manager manages more than one building for an owner, each building should have a separate operating budget. Usually, the operating budgets are tied to a calendar year, but a fiscal year can also be used. The budgets should be completed and presented to the owners for review at least three months before starting a new year. That should give the owners adequate time to consider the proposed budgets and give the property managers enough time to make any changes requested by the owners.

Different buildings may have different vacancy rates, bad debt ratios, and revenue sources, depending upon their locations, sizes and conditions. When preparing an operating budget, property managers will have to estimate the revenue generated by the building in the next year. They have to take several factors into consideration, including turnovers, vacancies, bad debts and rent increases.

When a tenant vacates, some time is required to clean and perform minor repairs on the unit before the new tenant moves in. Sometimes, the new tenant may also require the landlord to install some improvements in the unit, such as a window air conditioning unit. The time required to facilitate the move-out and move-in of tenants can be anywhere from one day to more than a week. During that period, there is no rental revenue, which is called a turnover loss. Property managers will have to estimate how many tenants may move out in the next year, the total time required for the turnover, and the potential loss of income accordingly.

Vacancy loss refers to the periods that the units remain unoccupied and there are no immediate tenant prospects, which creates a loss of income due to the vacancy. The vacancy periods may become longer or shorter next year due to several factors, such as increased or reduced competition, demand, change in the neighbourhood environment and other market conditions.

It is difficult to estimate how much bad debt will occur next year when a property manager prepares an operating budget. Bad debt happens when a tenant is delinquent in paying the rent and, for a variety of reasons, recovery of the rent is not possible. Possible reasons include personal bankruptcy of the tenant, unknown whereabouts of the tenant, or legal costs for attempted recovery are not justified. Property managers usually will base on the history of the building to project the bad debt amount next year. Grouping it with the vacancy loss is also a method to increase its accuracy.

The revenue next year can be increased by raising the current rent level. However, increasing the rent may cause some tenants to move out of the building if alternatives in the market offer a lower rent. Moreover, property managers must ensure such projections do not exceed the legal rent increase limit if there is rent control in the region.

A sample of the operating budget is shown in Appendix 7.

Capital Budget

A capital budget is used for long-term planning for a real estate investment. It may be used for studying the profitability of performing major renovations to improve the property. In such a case, significant funding will be required, and the owner may want to know the rate of return of the investment. When property managers prepare capital budgets, there are different factors that they have to consider. Usually, they have to know:

- the estimated capital cost for the work, including the cost of contractors and related professionals
- the amount and cost of financing required
- the loss of revenue (if any) during the period when work is being performed
- the life expectancy of the improvements after the works are completed
- the extra gross rental income that will be generated upon completion of the works
- the new assessed value of the buildings after the completion of the works, hence the increase in property taxes
- the estimated market value of the buildings upon completion of the works

When the above information is gathered or estimated, property managers may use different methods in capital budgeting to measure the return on investment, including the techniques such as:

- Overall Capitalization Rate
- Payback Period
- Net Present Value
- Internal Rate of Return
- Modified Internal Rate of Return
- Financial Management Rate of Return

Please refer to my other book[2] for detailed explanations of those methods.

Monthly Operating Statement

Property managers may need to prepare monthly operating statements for the owners to understand the performance of the building with the maintenance works done each month. The monthly operating statements will also be used to compare with the annual operating budget.

A monthly operating statement should specify the building address and for which month it is prepared. It should record the actual revenue and expenses for the current month and year-to-date and compare them to the budget amounts. The variance, either positive or negative, should also be calculated and reported.

---

[2] Law, Bryan. *Real Estate Investment: Theories and Analysis*, Fox College of Business, 2021.

The total annual budget for each category, both revenue and expenses, should also be included in a monthly operating statement. It can explain how the annual estimated expenses and revenue are compared to the monthly and year-to-date actual performance. Appendix 8 shows a sample operating statement as a reference.

7. Ethics and Risk Management

Ethics

Many property managers are members of professional bodies and have their association's code of ethics to follow. Even if they do not belong to any professional associations; they should perform their work ethically by protecting the owners' best interest and treating the tenants fairly and honestly as the minimum requirements.

A property management company may manage more than one building for different owners in the same neighbourhood. There will be a conflict of interest as the property managers of the same company will have to acquire tenants in the neighbourhood for different owners as the management agreements may be different. Suppose one property owner offers a bonus to the property manager if the building is over 95% rented in a year and the other building owner does not. In that case, the property management company may ask their managers to shift tenants to the building that offers a bonus and leave the other building with a higher vacancy rate.

Of course, suppose the property management company does that. In that case, neither the property managers nor the management company will survive in the marketplace when people find out that they engage in such unethical practices, which happens sooner or later.

<u>Misrepresentations</u>

To attract prospective tenants, property managers may have to advertise their properties with features and benefits. Some of them may be the facts; some may be overstated or misrepresented. Those are common problems in the advertising field, and property managers must pay attention to avoid making any mistakes.

Misrepresentations can be written or oral. It is usually a false statement or claim made by one party to another regarding some existing fact matter or circumstance affecting the contract or its purpose before or when the contract is concluded.

Misrepresentations can be innocent, negligent or fraudulent. An innocent misrepresentation happens when a party makes an untrue statement but honestly believes it is true. Suppose a victim of innocent misrepresentation is induced into a contract based on such a statement. In that case, the victim may refuse to complete the contract, attempt to set it aside or attempt to recover anything paid or delivered under the contract.

For example, a property management company advertises that the rent of a one-bedroom unit in its building is the lowest one in town. The rents of their one-bedroom units were the lowest in the area until there is a new triplex converted from a single-family house. The property management company failed to notice the existence of the triplex and made the statement. Consequently, a new tenant who just signed a lease may refuse to close the transaction after knowing the triplex offers a lower rent by arguing that a misrepresentation has occurred. However, the court may have the discretion to award damages instead of rescission of the lease.

A negligent misrepresentation happens between two parties in a relationship. One of them owes a duty of care to the other party, such as lawyers and their clients. The representation is made carelessly and in breach of duty; without reasonable care to ensure that the representation is accurate.

For example, a property management company acts as an agent of the owner of a property. When the owner sells the property, the buyer wants to confirm that all fridges and stoves are included in the price. The management company tells the owner that they belong to the owner without verifying that some of the appliances belong to the tenants. The buyer may claim damages due to the discrepancies in the number of appliances. Since the management company misleads the owner, the owner may claim damages from the company too. The victim of a negligent misrepresentation may claim both rescission and damages.

A misrepresentation is said to be fraudulent if a party made a false statement, which

- The party knew that the representation was false or that the party made the statement recklessly without knowledge of its truth;
- The misrepresentation was made with the intention that the other party would rely on it;
- The other party did rely on the misrepresentation to make a decision; and
- The other party suffered harm as a result of the misrepresentation.

For example, a property manager told a prospective tenant that the rental building was within the boundary of a famous school. Actually, the property manager knew that the building was outside the boundary. The prospective tenant rented a unit in the building and found out the fact after moving in. That is a fraudulent misrepresentation. Like negligent misrepresentation, the victim of a fraudulent misrepresentation may claim both rescission and damages. The party that made a fraudulent misrepresentation is subject to a criminal accusation.

To avoid misrepresentations, property managers should not make any statement without first finding out the facts. They should not cover any damages in the units to give them a better presentation. They should not promise what they cannot deliver, including those outside their authority. Property management companies should let their new property managers work with experienced managers for a period to get familiar with the buildings and procedures.

Landlord and Tenant Relationship

Maintaining a good landlord and tenant relationship is a crucial task for property managers. If the tenants can live in the building happily, the jobs of property managers can be done easier. The tenants' turnover rate will also be reduced, giving the owner a higher net profit which is one of the objectives of property managers.

An essential element of tenant relations is communication. The management should be reachable by the tenants for enquiries, complaints and assistance. Many problems and contentious issues between property managers and tenants arise due to misunderstandings of the lease. Another common reason is that many tenants feel they are not treated fairly or equally.

<u>Human Rights</u>

All tenants should be treated fairly and non-discriminatively. Different jurisdictions have different laws to protect human rights. Although not every government has detailed and well-covered human rights laws to protect their citizens, usually people are protected from discrimination against:

- Age
- Ancestry (colour and race)
- Citizenship
- Ethnic origin
- Place of origin

- Creed
- Disability
- Family status (have children or not)
- Marital status (including single status)
- Gender identity (including gender expression)
- Receipt of public assistance
- Sex (including pregnancy and breastfeeding)
- Sexual orientation

Property managers should not refuse a prospective tenant, harass a tenant, or treat a tenant unfairly because of one or more of the above grounds. Some property managers will use their discretion to give tenants flexibility for minor violations when dealing with rules and regulations. If they think such minor violations are acceptable, they should give all tenants the same flexibility regardless of their background. Otherwise, it will invite criticism and have the possibility of the allegation of discrimination. For more information regarding human rights, please refer to another book[3] of mine for reference.

Moving

When tenants move in or out, they may need assistance from the property managers. Some property management companies will provide a welcome kit to new tenants. The kit may consist of gadgets such as keychains,

---

[3] Law, Bryan. *Canadian Human Rights in a Nutshell*, Fox College of Business, 2020.

cardholders, sticky notes and fridge magnets. Usually, they are imprinted with the management company's name and info for advertising purposes. An information sheet, such as parking space allocation and instruction on using the security system, and other helpful community information such as a city map or bus route map, can also be added to the welcome kit. Such a welcome kit may give a good impression to the new tenants and help them settle in the neighbourhood. A good first impression is the first step to building up a good landlord-and-tenant relationship.

When a tenant moves in, the property manager should ensure that the keys, garage door remote control and security access cards are in working condition. The tenant should also be told their unit's buzz code and the functions of the intercom system. Suppose a building tour was not given to the new tenant before the moving date. In that case, the property manager should make sure that a tour can be scheduled as soon as possible so that the new tenant can be familiar with the locations and features of the facilities.

When a tenant moves out, it does not mean that it is the end of the landlord and tenant relationship. At least, it is not the end of promoting the general landlord and tenant relationship. The moved-out tenants would be the building ambassadors if they had a good experience when they lived in the building. Property managers should ask the moving-out tenants for their contact information to reach them, such as the ex-tenants having mail that needs forwarding.

Reducing Risks

Property managers must reduce the risk of litigations and insurance claims. It does not matter whether the property managers are the agents or employees of the owner; they represent the owner when dealing with the tenants. Therefore, they must watch what they say to the tenants and avoid any misrepresentation. On the other hand, they will also need to answer questions raised by the owner, such as the condition and the life expectance of the improvements. Property managers should not give opinions outside their expertise to the owners. Instead, they should simply provide information obtained from other professionals, such as engineers or equipment providers.

Property managers should never give advice to prospective tenants regardless of the subjects of the questions. Advising a prospective tenant may create, unintentionally, an implied or undisclosed agency relationship between the property manager and the prospective tenant. As the property manager represents the owner, that will make the property manager represents both parties and cause a dual agency relationship for the property manager. However, the property manager will only protect the best interest of the owner, such as negotiating the highest rent for the owner. That will cause legal liabilities to the property manager for not protecting the prospective tenant's best interest.

A disclosure and acknowledgement document may reduce the risk of misrepresentation and an unintentionally created dual-agency relationship. The disclosure document should state all the facts that are important to the tenants, which can be expanded, such as the school boundaries, transportation networks and other common issues in the neighbourhood. The acknowledgement document should state that the property manager is an agent of the owner and is not an agent of the tenant and that the tenant is free to seek professional advice before signing the lease.

Insurance

Buying insurance is one of the best ways to lower the risks in real estate investment. It can hedge the risk of contingent or uncertain loss. The most common type of insurance policy is fire insurance. If there is a fire that burnt down the property, fire insurance covers the replacement value of the property. Since the land cannot be burnt down, the replacement value is the estimated reconstruction costs of the improvements on the land.

Some owners will buy insurance for an insured value less than the replacement value to save the insurance premium. Property managers should make the owners know the importance of insurance and ensure that the insured value is enough for the replacement costs of the building, as it is the primary purpose of buying insurance. Fire insurance can only cover financial losses but cannot recover casualties. Property managers must try their best to reduce fire risk, including testing the fire alarms, and smoke and carbon monoxide detectors once a month.

Fire insurance is just the basic policy that property owners need to have. There are other coverages that property owners need, such as Third Party Liability and Water Damage. Some of them are included in a standard fire insurance policy but not always. Property managers must ensure they have proper insurance coverage according to the situation. Typical extended coverage protects various catastrophes, such as storms, hail, explosions, impact by aircraft or vehicles, and smoke.

Some common special coverages include Vandalism and Loss of Income. Since every building has visitors, that means it is open to the public. As a result, vandalism will be expected. Like most insurance policies, there is a deductible in vandalism policies, and the amount is usually high. In most instances, the cost of removal of graffiti or repair for minor damage is lower than the deductible. Therefore, the property managers will not file a claim to the insurance company and just repair it at their cost. It becomes part of the operating expenses. Still, insurance coverage for vandalism should be obtained as, on occasion, the cost of repair can be very expensive.

Loss of income coverage is essential to the owners, especially the owner of large buildings. When a building is subject to severe damage due to fire or other causes, some or all tenants may be required to leave their units until repairs are completed. The local tenancy law may absolve the tenants from paying rent until they can return to their units. It is therefore essential to have insurance to cover the loss of rental income during the repair period. That is especially important for owners who rely on rental incomes to pay for their mortgages.

As discussed in Chapter 3, tenants must be required to maintain an insurance policy that provides comprehensive general public liability insurance for the leased premises for not less than a certain amount and to cover their personal belongings in the unit.

Another type of insurance that property managers must buy is Professional Errors and Omissions insurance. It protects a property management company, its property managers and workers against claims of inadequate work or negligent actions. However, this type of insurance is not paid by the owners (from the trust accounts) and should be paid directly by the property management company.

Management Agreement

A formal property management agreement should always be signed if an owner wants to hire a third party to manage a building. It protects both the property manager and the owner by clearly listing out the work to be done by the property manager, the fee to be charged, and each party's roles and responsibilities.

A typical property management agreement contains the following elements:

- Parties to the agreement
- Property address and description
- Term of the property management contract
- Powers and duties granted within the agreement
- Property management fees and other fees

Appendix 9 shows a sample property management agreement for reference.

Appendix 1. Glossary in Property Management

(For both Commercial and Residential Property Management)

Abandonment: A surrender or relinquishment of real property, including a piece of land or a housing unit. Abandonment of leased premises refers to relinquishing the premises by the tenant without the owner's consent before the tenancy ends and without paying the rent.

Abatement: A reduction of rent, interest, or an amount due.

Acceptance: The act of accepting an offer made by a party.

Accounting: The theory and system that involves setting up and maintaining the book of a business or an entity; analyzing the operation of a business from a study of incomes and expenses.

Ad Valorem: A Latin term meaning "according to value" and is used to describe a tax that is levied against real property based on its value.

Adjustment: Often used in the law of insurance, the settlement of the amount to be received by the insured.

Affidavit of Service: A formal statement made under oath

Affordable Housing: Housing projects governed by the government or its agency to offer affordable rental units to people when they meet specific criteria.

Agency Management: Property management by an agency, authorized and appointed by the property owner.

Agent: A person who has a legal basis to act on behalf of another person to deal with a third party.

Aggregate Rent: The total or gross rent amount for a lease term.

Agreement Date: The date that the landlord and the tenant sign the lease.

Alteration: The process of changing the function of a property.

Amortization: It is the process of spreading out a loan into a series of equal payments, and the loan is paid off at the end of the payment schedule.

Amenities: Desirable or useful features or facilities of a building or place that increase its value or make it more desirable.

Anchor Tenant: A key tenant in a shopping centre that will attract other businesses as well as shoppers.

Annual Statement: A detailed and annotated statement of all income and expense items covers a twelve-consecutive-month period of operation of a property.

Apartment: A residential unit inside a structure built forming one residence, typically in a building containing a number of these.

Apartment Building: A building designed for separate apartments, usually a mid-rise or high-rise building.

Appraisal: An estimate of value. A formal report for that purpose.

Assessment: The estimation of the value of properties for the purposes of charging taxes.

Asset: Any property or right with a monetary value.

Asset Management: A sophisticated form of property management under which the management organizes, operates, and assumes the risk of the total real estate business venture and whose concern extends beyond net operating income.

Assignment: The act of a tenant to let a third party take over an existing lease and become the tenant.

Automatic Renewal: A lease provision that automatically ensures the renewal of the lease unless either the tenant or the landlord notifies the other party of a desire to terminate the tenancy.

Balloon Payment: The final payment of a loan that is considerably larger than the required periodic payments. Most balloon loans require one large payment that pays off the remaining balance at the end of the loan term. It may also refer to the payment of all rents payable for the remaining lease term.

Base Rent: The minimum amount of rent payable under the terms of a commercial lease, also known as Minimum Rent and Net Rent.

Base-Unit-Approach: A method of establishing rental rates where a typical unit within a specific submarket is defined and becomes the standard for measuring all similar units.

Blanket Mortgage: A single mortgage loan covering several pieces of property.

Blanket Policy: A single insurance policy that covers all of a specified quantity or class of property, a variety of risks, or both.

Board of Directors: The official governing body of a corporation usually refers to condominiums and cooperatives.

Broker: A professional in the real estate sector, usually licensed, who trades on behalf of others while receiving a commission in the process.

Budget: A prediction of income and expenses over a specific time period for a particular property.

Building Codes: Ordinances specifying minimum standards of construction of buildings to protect public safety and health.

Bulk User: A commercial enterprise that utilizes a large quantity of office space.

Bylaws: Regulations that provide specific procedures for handling routine matters, such in as a city, a condominium or a cooperative.

Capitalization: The process of converting a property's anticipated future income into value.

Cashier: The position in a property management firm that records all income, bills accounts, and draws buildings' payrolls.

Capitalization Rate: It is a rate of return to measure the investment's potential and profitability. The formula is Net Income ÷ Price and is usually shortened as Cap Rate.

Cede: To assign or transfer.

Cash Flow: The amount of cash available after all payments have been made for operating expenses and mortgage payments.

Chattel: A movable article of property other than land, buildings, or improvements legally and physically annexed or attached to real property.

Commencement Date: The date upon which the lease term starts and rental begins to accrue; usually, it is also the day the tenant takes possession but not necessarily.

Common Area: Space that is not used and occupied exclusively by tenants, such as concourse, elevators, and stairways. In a condominium complex, it refers to space shared by the unit owners.

Common Area Maintenance Clause: A provision in commercial leases that states the tenant must pay a share of the cost of operating and maintaining the common area of the property.

Comparables: The similar properties that are used to determine the value of a property. It is done by comparing the sold prices of the comparable with the subject property to indicate the expected sale price.

Condominium: A housing project with multiple single-family units such that each unit can be owned by different individuals or entities.

Controllable Expense: An operating expense over which property managers have definite responsibility and control.

Cooperative: An ownership of real estate through the ownership of interest or share in a corporation, with or without equity.

Corporation: A form of business organization created by statute law and considered a separate legal entity.

Corrective Maintenance: Ongoing repairs that must be made to a building and its equipment to maintain its use and value.

Cosigner: A secondary signer on a lease or mortgage who provides additional assurance to the landlord or lender.

Curb Appeal: A concept expressing the attractiveness of the property's visual look as viewed from the street level.

Custodial Maintenance: Cleaning and maintenance tasks including carpentry, electrical, plumbing and HVAC repair and maintenance.

Debt Service: The amount of money paid to a loan or a mortgage to service the debt.

Deferred Maintenance: Ordinary maintenance that is not performed to a building and its equipment on time such that it may negatively affect a property's use and value.

Deficiency Discount: A reduction in rent to induce a tenant to accept a substandard apartment.

Deed: An instrument in writing that conveys a title or an interest in real property.

Demised Premises: Space covered by a lease agreement.

Depreciation: Loss of value of a physical asset resulting from the loss of functionality, economic obsolescence, or physical deterioration.

Devise: To assign or transmit real property by will.

Duplex: A house built to include two separate dwellings within the same structure.

Easement: A right or interest in land entitles another landowner to use, privilege, or benefit from or over said land.

Economic Life: The period of time for which a building can be used to produce income or services.

Effective Gross Income: The potential income from all real property operations after an allowance is made for a vacancy and bad debt losses.

Encumbrance: An outstanding claim or a lien recorded against real property or any legal right to the use of the property by another party who is not the owner of that property.

Equity: A difference between the home's market value and the monetary amount owed to the lender who holds the mortgage.

Escalation Clause: A provision in a lease that guarantees automatic rent increase within the lease term.

Ethics: A system of applied moral principles that govern property managers' behaviour and decisions.

Eviction: A legal process for the removal of a tenant from their current home.

Eviction Notice: A legal notice from the landlord that describes the tenant's default connected to the lease terms. Eviction notices aim to inform tenants of a pending eviction applied against them.

Exclusive Right: The right for one tenant exclusively to conduct a specific business in the leased property.

Fair Market Value: At a specific time, the price that an asset would sell for on the open market with neither buyer nor seller is under any compulsion to act.

Fee Simple Ownership: The highest possible form and most absolute ownership of land, subject to the least number of restrictions.

Fixed Expenses: The expenses that do not vary with the occupancy rate and are independent of the rental income.

Flat Fee: A monthly or yearly property management fee in a dollar amount.

Fixture: An article attached permanently to a building or land to become part of the real estate.

Fixturing Period: The rent-free period offered to commercial tenants to renovate their units, especially for retail space.

Furnishings: Furniture, appliances, and other chattels used in a unit.

Garnishment: A legal process for collecting a monetary judgment on behalf of a plaintiff from a defendant. Garnishment allows the plaintiff to take the money or property of the debtor from the person or institution that holds that property.

Gross Floor Area: The total floor area, including the common area.

Gross Leasable Area: The total floor area designed for tenants' occupancy and exclusive use in a commercial property.

Gross Lease: A lease agreement in which the tenant pays a fixed rent, and the owner pays all the expenses associated with operating the property.

Ground Lease: A long-term lease for vacant land on which the tenant usually is required to build their own building as specified by the lease.

Holdover Tenant: A tenant retains possession of the leased premises after the lease has expired.

HVAC: Heating, Ventilating, and Air-Conditioning; a unit combined of heating, ventilation, and air conditioning to regulate the temperature indoors.

Landlord: An owner of a property or the appointed agent receives payments from tenants taking space in the rental unit.

Landlord Insurance: An insurance policy covering the landlord from financial losses associated with their rental property, such as theft and fire.

Lease: A contract outlining the terms and conditions between a landlord and tenant for the possession of the real property for a specified time and in exchange for fixed payments.

Leasehold: The holding of real property under a lease.

Lease Renewal: The continuation of the lease after its initial expiration.

Lease Term: The fixed time period for a tenancy.

Leasing Agent: An agent who leases real estate properties and signs the leases on behalf of the owner.

Lessee: The tenant.

Lessor: The landlord.

Life Estate: An interest in property that continues for an individual's life and terminates in favour of others in the event of his death.

Life Lease: A form of tenancy arrangement gives the leaseholder a right to reside in the property for an extended period of time, usually not less than 50 years and commonly for the life lease holder's whole lifetime.

Management Agreement: A written contract in which a property owner contracts the management of a property to an individual manager or a firm and details all parties' rights and obligations.

Management Fee: Monetary consideration paid to property managers for the performance of management duties, usually a percentage of the net operating income.

Ma-Pa Management: The management of real property by a couple where typically the wife assumes the duties of renting and record-keeping and the husband performs the maintenance tasks.

Market Approach: Estimating a property's value by comparing it with similar properties that have been rented or sold recently.

Mobile Home: A factory-manufactured dwelling that often is located on a leased lot and connected to local utilities.

Month-to-Month Tenancy: A tenancy for consecutive and continuing monthly periods until terminated by either the landlord or the tenant with proper notice.

Mortgage: A conditional pledge of property to a lender as security against a debt.

Mortgagee: The lender of a mortgage.

Mortgagor: The borrower of a mortgage.

Net Lease: A lease in which the tenant pays base rent and all the expenses connected with the leased premises.

Net Operating Income (NOI): The rental income remaining after operating expenses have been deducted from the effective gross income.

Off-Site Management: The management of real properties by persons not residing or keeping office hours at the subject property.

Operating Budget: A financial plan predicting the property's income and expenses over a period of time.

Operating Expenses: All expenses necessary to maintain the production of income from the operation of a property.

Percentage Rent: Rent charged in retail space that is based on a percentage of the gross sales of the tenant.

Potential Gross Income: The rental income of a property based on the assumption that it is 100% rented.

Preventive Maintenance: A program of regular inspection and maintenance that prevents potential problems.

Principal: A person who appoints another individual as an agent to deal with a third party on behalf of that person.

Property Manager: A person or company managing real estate properties according to the owners' objectives.

Property Taxes: A tax based on the property's value to be paid by the property owner to the local government.

Radius Clause: A provision in a retail lease under which a tenant agrees not to own or operate another store within a specified distance of that retail property.

Real Estate Cycle: A cycle of the real estate market is composed of four main phases, including recovery, expansion, hyper-supply, and recession.

Rent Guarantee Insurance (Rent Default Insurance): An insurance covering the landlord if a renter defaults on rental payments or the property is damaged and cannot be rented out.

Rent Concessions: Things conceded or granted to induce the making of a lease.

Rent Control: Government regulations imposed on residential properties to limit the increase in rents.

Rent Roll: A register of rents showing the tenants' names, their unit numbers, the amount due, and the total rental income received.

Rentable Area: The usable area of a tenant, plus an apportioned allocation of common areas.

Rental Ledger: A document recording tenants' names, their units, phone numbers, rents, security deposits, and other rental information.

Rental Schedule: A list of rental rates of the units in a rental building.

Renter Insurance: An insurance policy that mainly covers a tenant's personal properties and liabilities.

Retrofit: The replacement or upgrade of some fixtures or facilities in a building to comply with the latest requirements (usually related to fire regulations).

Return on Investment (ROI): A metric that measures the performance of an investment as a percentage of the investment capital.

Right of Re-entry: The act of resuming possession of the real property. Most jurisdictions have regulations regarding how to proceed.

Security Deposit: A refundable payment collected from the tenant by the landlord to cover possible damages and ensure faithful performance of the lease by the tenant.

Subletting: Renting a property by a tenant to a third party (the subtenant) for a specified segment of the tenant's lease agreement.

Tenant Application: An application form that has to be filled out by a prospective tenant in case of interest for a particular rental property, usually with authorization to perform a check of credit on that tenant.

Tenant Damages: Any damage occurring during the lease term that is not considered normal wear and tear.

Tenant Screening: A process carried out by the landlord to verify the background of a potential tenant, usually including a credit check, interviews, and background check.

Tenancy at Sufferance: A tenant continues to occupy a rental property after the lease expiration, and the owner does not authorize it (also referred to as an overholding tenancy).

Tenancy at Will: A tenant has no lease but occupies the property under the owner's consent.

Tenant Mix: The broad representation of businesses that comprise a commercial building; of households that comprise a multifamily building.

Term Lease: The specified time that a tenancy is bound.

Termination Date: The date upon which the lease term ends, rentals cease to accrue, and the tenant gives up possession to the landlord.

Turnkey Property: A rental property that requires no urgent repair or update by the buyer and can immediately be rented out after purchase.

Turnover: The number of units that are vacated during a specific period of time, one month or one year, usually expressed as a ratio between the number of units vacated and the total number of units in a building.

Usable Area: The total interior area within the walls of the tenant space.

Vacancy Rate: The ratio of vacant rental units to the total number of rental units in a building, city or region.

Appendix 2. Sample Tenancy Agreement

TENANCY AGREEMENT

This Agreement dated the **2nd day of April 2021** is made pursuant to the provision of the **Local Residential Tenancy Act** and amendments thereto.

BETWEEN: John Roe   **(Landlord)**

AND: **Jane Doe and Peter Doe (Tenant)**

1. RENTED PREMISES
The Landlord agrees to rent to the Tenant, hereinafter referred to as the "Premises", at **123 Main Street, Major City, Any State, USA.**

2. TERM
The Tenant agrees to occupy the Premises, subject to the present occupant vacating and subject to the Premises being available for occupancy, for a term of **one** year beginning on the **1st day of May 2021** and ending on the **30th day of April 2021**.

3. USE OF PREMISES
The Tenant agrees to use the Premises as a single-family residential dwelling and for no other purposes, to abide by the covenants, agreements, rules and regulations of this

Agreement and not to allow the Premises to be occupied by anyone other than the persons listed hereunder,

Name: **Peter Doe**   Relationship: **Son**
Name: **Mary Doe**   Relationship: **Daughter**

4. RENT
The Tenant(s) agrees to pay the total monthly rent to the Landlord in advance on the **1st** day of each month during the term of this Agreement, at Landlord's office or at such place as the Landlord may from time to time direct, as follows:

Monthly Rent: **$1,200.00**
Rents are payable to: **John Roe**   (Landlord)

5. PRORATED RENT
The Tenant agrees to pay a prorated rent of **$800.00** in advance to cover the period of occupancy from the **11th day of April 2021** to the **30th day of April 2021**. The occupancy during this period is subject to the terms and conditions of this Tenancy Agreement.

6. PREPAID RENT
The Tenant agrees to deposit with the Landlord the sum of $2,400.00 as prepaid rent to be applied towards the **First** AND the last month's rent of the term of this Agreement or the last month's rent of any renewal agreement. The Tenant agrees that upon the renewal of each and every term, he will deposit with the Landlord the amount of the increased rent of the new rental term.

7. UTILITIES

The Tenant agrees to set up an account and pay to the local utility directly for the following services applicable to the Premises:

Heat _____ Hydro _____ Water _____ Telephone _____
Cable _____ Internet _____ Others: _____

8. ASSIGNMENT AND SUBLET

The Tenant agrees not to assign or sublet the Premises without Landlord's written consent; such consent shall not be arbitrarily or unreasonably withheld. The Tenant agrees to pay for an administration and processing fee provided that this shall not be construed to mean automatic acceptance of a prospective assignee or subtenant who would otherwise have been accepted as a tenant and provided that any acceptable assignee or subtenant shall enter into a Tenancy Agreement directly with the Landlord for a term not less than the unexpired portion of this Agreement.

9. CARE OF PREMISES

The Landlord covenants to keep the Premises in a good state of repair, and the Tenant agrees to give the Landlord prompt written notice of any accident or other defect in the water pipes, heating apparatus, wiring or any other part of the Premises. The Tenant covenants to maintain, keep and leave the Premises in an ordinary state of cleanliness, and repair any damage caused to the Premises by his willful or negligent conduct or that of persons who are permitted on the Premises. Tenant further agrees to have all evidence of animal/bird remedied professionally at Tenant's own expense before vacating the premises. All appliances are free for the Tenant to use and should not be used as a ground for abatement of rent if they are out of order.

10. CONDITION OF PREMISES

The Tenant further agrees that there was no promise made by the Landlord with respect to any alteration, remodelling or decoration of the Premises or installation of equipment or fixtures in the Premises except such, if any, as is expressly set out in this Agreement. No representation or undertaking has been made by the Landlord except as set out in this Agreement.

11. FIRE

The Tenant covenants not to do or permit anything to be done in the Premises or its environs, or bring or keep anything therein which will in any way create a risk of fire or increase in the rate of fire insurance on the building or content. When a fire originates within the Premises, the Tenant is responsible for the damages, and the Tenant agrees to pay and maintain adequate liability insurance for payment of repairs and all related claims.

(a) The Tenant agrees with the Landlord that he will, in case of fire, give immediate notification of the same to the Landlord.

(b) The Tenant acknowledges that the Landlord has affixed in the Premises a certain smoke-detecting device in accordance with the bylaws of the City. The Tenant covenants not to remove or willfully damage the smoke detectors and maintain the battery in the said smoke detectors, including, at his expense, immediately replacing the battery as often as necessary for the proper operation of the devices. The Tenant further agrees to immediately advise the Landlord of any malfunction of such devices as a result of the failure or non-replacement of batteries. The Tenant shall indemnify and save harmless the Landlord from any and all liability, damage, cost, claims and causes of actions whatsoever arising as a result of the Tenant's failure to comply with the aforementioned obligations.

(c) The Tenant agrees that he will indemnify the Landlord and any other Resident of the building against any loss, cost or damage because of any neglect, carelessness or injury caused by him or any of his family or household, or any guest or other person in the Premises.

12. No SMOKING

The tenant agrees and acknowledges that this is a smoke-free building.

a) No tenant, resident, guest, visitor and business invitee, or visitor shall smoke cigarettes, cigars, water pipe, or any similar product whose use generates smoke within the building. This prohibition includes all residential units within the building, all balconies and patios, enclosed common areas, as well as outside within 9 metres of doorways, operable windows and air intakes.

b) "Smoking" shall include the inhaling, exhaling, or burning of any tobacco, cannabis or similar product whose use generates smoke.

c) "Business invitee" shall include but is not limited to any contractor, agent, household worker, personal support worker, or other person hired by the tenant or resident to provide a service or product to the tenant or resident.

13. LOCKS

The Tenant agrees not to change or install any lock in the Premises without the prior written consent of the Landlord; such consent shall not be unreasonably withheld. In the event that a lock is changed or installed, the Tenant agrees to immediately provide the Landlord with a key to the new lock at his own expense.

14. RULES AND REGULATIONS

The Tenant agrees to comply with all the terms as set out in Schedule "A" of the Offer to Lease (if there is any), each of the bylaws, rules and regulations of the Condominium Corporation (if this rental unit is a condominium unit), and such other bylaws, rules and regulations as may from time to time be amended, modified or added upon written or posted a notice to the Tenant by the landlord or the Condominium Corporation (if it applies).

15. RIGHT OF ENTRY

The Tenant agrees that the Landlord shall be entitled to enter the Premises under the **Local Residential Tenancy Act** to view the state of repair and make such repairs and alternations as necessary. The tenant agrees that the premises would be inspected by the Landlord or his agent at least four times a year to make sure that the maintenance work could be done promptly.

16. LANDLORD'S PROPERTY

Drapes, blinds, carpeting, broadloom, appliances, or other similar fixtures provided by the Landlord shall not be removed or disconnected from windows, walls, floors, or electric circuits of the Premises without the prior written consent of the Landlord.

17. SYSTEMS

In the event of a breakdown of the electrical, mechanical, heating or plumbing systems, the Landlord shall not be liable for damages or personal discomfort caused by such breakdown. However, the Landlord will carry out repairs with reasonable diligence.

18. PROPERTY TAXES

The Landlord shall pay all real property taxes with respect to the Premises as assessed against the Landlord. If the Tenant wishes to change the assessment with respect to school taxes, the Tenant agrees to pay the increased cost resulting from the change.

19. INSURANCE

The Tenant shall solely be responsible for his personal property located in the rented premises and shall obtain and be responsible for his own insurance coverage for liability and personal content for not less than one million dollars ($1,000,000.00). **The Tenant shall provide to the Landlord with evidence that all such policies are in place and in effect and showing a photo ID as conditions for the Tenant to receive unit keys on the lease commencement day**.

20. FURNITURE AND PERSONAL EFFECT

Any furniture and personal effects found in or about the Leased Premises after the Resident has vacated, abandoned or been evicted from there may be removed by the Landlord and may be disposed of as the Landlord sees fit. The Tenant shall pay the Landlord the amount of any costs incurred by him to remove and dispose of any such furniture and personal effects.

21. PETS

The Tenant agrees that he will not permit any dog, cat, or other animals, bird, insect, or reptile to be kept or allowed on, in, or about the Premises or its environs. Service animals are excepted.

22. FRUSTRATION OF CONTRACT

The Landlord and Tenants mutually covenant and agree that if during any term of this Agreement or any renewal thereof, the Premises shall be wholly or partially destroyed by fire or the elements (other than by the action of neglect of the Tenant) such as to render the Premises wholly or partially unfit for occupancy, then, until such damage shall be repaired, the rent shall abate in the proportion that the parts of the said Premises unfit for occupancy bear to the whole Premises. The Landlord shall repair same with all reasonable speed. The notice of the Landlord shall fix conclusively the date on which full rent shall recommence.

23. LIABILITY

The Landlord shall not in any event whatsoever be liable for or be responsible for:

(a) any personal injury or death that may be suffered or sustained by the Tenant or any employee of the Tenant or any member of the Tenant's family, his agents or guests, or any other person who may be upon the Premises or the Premises of the Landlord; or

(b) any loss of or damage or injury to any property including cars and contents thereof belonging to the Tenant or to any member of the Tenant's family, his agents or guests, or to any other person who may be upon the Premises or the Premises of the Landlord; or

(c) without limiting the generality of the foregoing, any damages to any such property caused by steam, rain, water or snow which may leak into, issue or flow from any part of the Premises or the Premises of the Landlord or from the water, steam, sprinkler or drainage pipes or plumbing works of the same or from any other place or quarter; or

(d) any damage caused by or attributable to the condition or arrangement of any electrical or other wiring systems; or

(e) any damage caused by anything done or omitted to be done by any tenant of the Landlord.

It is understood and agreed that the Tenant shall be solely responsible for his personal property located in the Premises.

24. NOTICE OF TERMINATION

In the event that either party wishes to terminate this Tenancy at the end of the term created by this Agreement, then he shall give notice to that effect in writing not less than sixty (60) days prior to the expiration of this Agreement.

(a) In the event that either party has given such notice (or any notice terminating the Tenancy created by clause (b) hereunder), the Premises may be shown to prospective tenants and purchasers at all reasonable hours.

(b) If no such notice pursuant to this paragraph has been delivered by either party, then the Tenant shall become a monthly Tenant under the terms and conditions herein set out, providing that nothing herein shall prevent the parties from agreeing to any other terms for said monthly Tenancy.

(c) In the event that the Tenant is obligated to vacate the Premises on or before a specific date, and the Landlord enters into a Tenancy Agreement with a third party, and the Tenant fails to vacate the Premises on or before the due date, thereby causing the Landlord to be liable to such third party, then the Tenant will (in addition to all liability to the Landlord for such overholding) indemnify the Landlord for all losses suffered thereby.

(d) Vacancy is to be given to the Landlord not later than 2:00 p.m. on the final day of this Tenancy, or any renewal thereof unless otherwise agreed upon in writing between the Landlord and the Tenant.

(e) When all contents of the Tenant have been removed from the Premises, the Tenant shall arrange with the Landlord or his duly authorized agent to complete an "Outgoing Inspection" Report which shall be signed by both parties (Tenant to retain one copy).

(f) Notwithstanding the term of this Agreement, both parties agree that in the event the Landlord sells the Premises, the Tenant agrees to allow vacant possession to the Purchaser, providing the Purchaser or the Vendor or the Agent for the Purchaser or Vendor gives the Tenant a Notice in Writing of not less than sixty (60) days prior to the end of any month that possession is required. The Tenant agrees to move on or before the date requested.

25. MITIGATION OF DAMAGES

The Landlord and Tenant mutually covenant and agree that when the Tenant abandons or vacates the Premises in breach of this Agreement or any renewal thereof, the Landlord is obligated to mitigate his damages. If the rent due is unpaid after the date on which it should have been paid, the Landlord as Agent of the Tenant may enter the Premises and, in addition to all other rights reserved to the Landlord, remove any effects found therein and re-rent the Premises and apply rent derived from there against the rent due under this

Tenancy Agreement or the renewal. For the purpose of this Tenancy Agreement, the Premises shall be deemed to have been vacated if the inspection done by the Landlord or his agent reveals the Premises to be substantially barren of the Tenant's furnishings and/or effects, and the Premises shall be deemed to have been abandoned if the Tenant fails to acknowledge the Landlord's written communication for a continuous period of seven (7) days during which rent due remains unpaid.

26. ILLEGAL ACT

The Tenant agrees, at any time during the term of the Agreement or any renewal thereof, not to exercise or carry on, or permit to be exercised or carried on, in or upon the Premises or any part thereof, any trade, business, occupation, calling, or illegal act.

27. BANKRUPTCY

Should the Tenant become bankrupt or insolvent, the immediately following three (3) months rent shall become due and payable, and this Agreement or any renewal thereof may at the option of the Landlord be immediately terminated.

28. BREACH OF COVENANT

Should the Landlord or the Tenant be in breach of any covenant herein provided (except paying the rent), the other party shall be required to give written notice of such breach within thirty (30) days of such breach coming to his attention and provide to the offending party a reasonable period within which to remedy such breach. Provided further that if such breach is remedied, there shall be no further liability for the breach and provided further that if no such notice is given, neither party shall have any remedy for the said alleged breach.

29. NOTICES

Except when otherwise provided by the Tenant Protection Act, any notice required or contemplated by any provision of this Agreement shall be deemed to be sufficiently given if served personally, or deemed to be received within seventy-two (72) hours of mailing post prepaid in any one of Her Majesty's Post Offices within the Province of Ontario, in a registered letter addressed to the Landlord as set forth herein, or to the Tenant at the address of the Premises.

30. TENANT'S WARRANTY

The Tenant hereby warrants that he is of the full age of eighteen (18) years, that he has read and understands this Agreement and that all information and particulars were explained to him by the Landlord or his duly authorized agent.

31. DISHONORED CHEQUES

In the event that any of the Tenant's cheque to the Landlord or his agent is dishonoured, the Tenant shall pay to the Landlord forthwith, in addition to the amount of the cheque, a collection charge of **$25.00** for such cheque so dishonoured.

32. GOVERNING LAW

This Agreement shall be governed by and construed in accordance with the laws of **Any State**. Should any provision or provisions of the Lease be illegal or not enforceable, it or they shall be considered separate and savable from the Lease, and its remaining provisions shall remain in force and be binding upon the parties hereto as thought the said provisions had never been included.

33. PROVISIONS
This Agreement and its acceptance are to be read with all changes of gender and number as may be required by the context. In the event of a conflict between any provision written or typed in the Agreement and any provision in the printed portion hereof, the written or typed provision shall supersede the printed provisions to the extent of such conflict.

Everything contained within this Agreement shall extend to and be binding on the respective heirs, executors, administrators, and successors of each party hereto. All covenants being contained shall be deemed joint and several.

SIGNED, SEALED
and DELIVERED
in the presence of

IN WITNESS whereof
I have hereunto set my
hand and seal:

_____   _____   _____

(Witness)   (Landlord / Agent)   (Date)

SIGNED, SEALED   IN WITNESS whereof
and DELIVERED   I have hereunto set my
in the presence of   hand and seal:

_____   _____ ✸ _____
(Witness)   (Tenant)   (Date)

_____   _____ ✸ _____
(Witness)   (Tenant)   (Date)

RECEIPT OF TENANCY AGREEMENT

I, THE UNDERSIGNED, hereby acknowledge this date having
received a duplicate original of the Tenancy Agreement.

_____   _____
(Tenant)   (Date)

_____   _____
(Tenant)   (Date)

Appendix 3. Sample Tenant Application Form

Rental Property Address:

_____

1. Applicant

Name: _____

S.I.N.: _____ Birthday : _____

2. Present Address

_____

_____

Tel :_____ How long: _____

3. Previous Address

_____

_____

Tel :_____ How long: _____

4. Driver's Licence

Number: _____

Expiry Date: _____ State: _____

5. Employer

Name: _____

Address: _____

Kind of Work: _____

Length of Employment: _____ Income: _____

Supervisor: _____ Phone #: _____

6. Spouse's Employer

Name: _____

Address: _____

Kind of Work: _____

Length of Employment: _____ Income: _____

Supervisor: _____ Phone #: _____

7. Name, Age and Relationship of All Occupants

Name: _____

Age: _____ Relationship: _____

Name: _____

Age: _____ Relationship: _____

Name: _____

Age: _____ Relationship: _____

Name: _____

Age: _____ Relationship: _____

8. Type of Vehicle

Brand: _____ Model: _____ Year: _____

License Plate #: _____ State: _____

Brand: _____ Model: _____ Year: _____

License Plate #: _____ State: _____

9. Pet

Will a pet be kept in the premises? _____

Kind/wieght/breed/age: _____

10. Your Bank

Name: _____

Address: _____

Account Number: _____

Name: _____

Address: _____

Account Number: _____

11. Reason(s) for Leaving Your Present Residence

_____

_____

_____

12. Present Landlord

Name: _____

Address: _____

Phone Number: _____

Length of Occupancy: _____

13. Previous Landlord

Name: _____

Address: _____

Phone Number: _____

Length of Occupancy: _____

14. Reference

Name: _____

Phone Number: _____

Name: _____

Phone Number: _____

15. Person to be contacted in case of emergency

Name: _____

Phone Number: _____

Address: _____

_____

I, _____, hereby certify that the above information is true and correct. I consent the Landlord or his Agent to perform a check of credit for/on my behalf.

Applicant's Signature

_____   _____
Signature   Date

Appendix 4. Sample Record of Inspection

PROPERTY ADDRESS:

_____

DATE OF INSPECTION:

_____

Kitchen:	Condition	Comments
Stove		
Refrigerator		
Dishwasher		
Light Fixtures		
Exhaust Fan		
Blinds & Drapes		
Ceiling		
Walls and Trims		
Floorings		
Others		
Living Room:	**Condition**	**Comments**
Light Fixtures		
Ceiling		
Walls and Trims		
Floorings		
Others		
Dining Room:	**Condition**	**Comments**
Light Fixtures		

Ceiling		
Walls and Trims		
Floorings		
Others		
Primary Bedroom:	**Condition**	**Comments**
Light Fixtures		
Ceiling		
Walls and Trims		
Floorings		
Others		
Second Bedroom:	**Condition**	**Comments**
Light Fixtures		
Ceiling		
Walls and Trims		
Floorings		
Others		
Extra Room:	**Condition**	**Comments**
Light Fixtures		
Ceiling		
Walls and Trims		
Floorings		
Others		

Other comments:

_____

_____

_____

_____

_____

_____

_____

_____

_____

NOTE: The tenant shall have three (3) days from the date of commencing occupancy to report to the Landlord regarding any discrepancy on the appliances included in this rental and the plumbing and electrical systems in the unit, failing which the tenant shall become solely responsible for the maintenance of all items as stipulated in the Lease.

Inspected and agreed by: _____

_____   _____

Tenant Signature   Date

Accompanied by landlord's agent: _____

_____   _____

Agent Signature   Date

Appendix 5. Sample Tenant Receipt of Keys

TENANT RECEIPT OF KEYS

Property Address:

_____

I, the undersigned, acknowledge receipt of the following
regarding the rental of the above property:

Number of keys   Cost for an additional set
                                                    /Replacement per set

__ set(s) of mail box key   _____
__ set(s) of suite key   _____
__ set(s) of locker key   _____
__ set(s) of garage door entrance key   _____
__ set(s) of recreation room entrance key   _____
__ set(s) of main door entrance key   _____
__ set(s) of remote control for garage door opener   _____
__ set(s) of main entrance access card/fob   _____
__ set(s) of _____   _____
__ set(s) of _____   _____

_____   SETS IN TOTAL

I shall be responsible for the safekeeping of the above items,
and I shall return them to the Landlord or his agent in good
condition upon termination of the lease. Costs for an

additional set(s) or replacement in case of loss or damage shall be at my expense.

Dated at _____ this ___ day of _____, 20_____.

_____   _____

Tenant's Signature   Date

_____   _____

Tenant's Signature   Date

REMARK:

_____

_____

_____

_____

Appendix 6. Sample Maintenance Checklist

BUILDING MAINTENANCE CHECKLIST

ITEM	DATE	REMARKS
Exterior		
Entrance and Emergency Door		
Walls		
Chalking and Paints		
Foundation		
Roof		
Gutter and Downspouts		
Chimney		
Porch and Deck		
Outdoor Stairs		
Yard		
Gardening		
Garbage & Recycling Area		
Parking Lot		
Garage		
Fences		
Concrete and Asphalt		
Lightings		
Others		
Interior		
Walls and Ceilings		
Floors		
Windows		
Doors		
Elevators		
Stairs		
Fire and Smoke Alarms		
CO Detectors		

Electrical Systems		
Mechanical Systems		
Plumbing Systems		
Heating and AC Systems		
Water Heater		
Lightings		
Others		

Appendix 7. Sample Operating Budget

Operating Budget - 2022

Property: 123 Main Street, Main Town.

For the period *01/01/2022 to 12/31/2022*	
Revenue	
Current Rental Income (2021)	$2,225,816
Rent Increase in 2022	$43,084
Gross Revenue	**$2,268,900**
Estimated Losses	
Minus: Turnover Loss (1%)	$22,689
Minus: Vacancy Loss (2%)	$45,378
Minus: Bad Debt (1%)	$22,689
Adjusted Revenue	**$2,178,144**
Extra Income	
Plus: Parking	$61,200
Plus: Coin Laundry	$30,400
Plus: Vending Machines	$2,600
EFFECTIVE REVENUE	**$2,272,344**

Expenses	
Utilities	
Electricity	$212,056
Gas	$120,648
Internet	$1,080
Telephone	$768
Water	$8,562
Total Utilities	**$343,114**
Administration	
Audit	$2,560
Insurance	$109,650

Paralegal	$1,680
Property Taxes	$166,520
Stationery and Sundry	$1,156
Management Fee	$95,000
Total Administration	**$376,566**
Repairs & Maintenance	
Air Conditioning	$2,400
Appliance	$1,500
Cleaning Supplies	$800
Common Area	$43,500
Elevator	$6,800
Fire and Safety	$2,210
Garage	$2,800
Garbage Collection	$6,850
Landscaping	$5,420
Light Fixtures	$1,050
Mechanical	$1,365
Plumbing	$1,550
Snow Removal	$8,250
Miscellaneous	$1,000
Reserve Fund	$66,500
Total Repairs & Maintenance	**$151,995**
TOTAL EXPENSES	**$871,675**
CASH FLOW BEFORE DEBT SERVICE	**$1,400,669**

Appendix 8. Sample Operating Statement

Monthly Operating Statement

Address: _____

For the month of _____, 20_____

Item	Current Month			Year to Date			Annual Budget
	Actual	Budget	Variance	Actual	Budget	Variance	
Revenue							
Rent							
Parking							
Laundry							
Recoveries							
Total							
Expenses							
Electricity							
Gas							
Water							
Maintenance							
Repair							
Garbage							
Gardening							
Snow Removal							
Professional Fees							
Management Fee							
Total							
Net Profit							

Appendix 9. Sample Management Agreement

Property Management Agreement

This Property Management Agreement (the "Agreement") is made this _____ day of _____, 20___ (the "Effective Date"), by and between _____, (the "Owner") and _____, (the "Manager"), also individually referred to as "Party", and collectively "the Parties." The Parties agree as follows:

1.0 Purposes

1.1 The Owner owns the property located at _____ (the "Property"). The Manager is in the business of managing properties of this type. The Owner desires to engage the Manager to manage the Property, more fully described in Section 3.0 ("Services") hereof, for and in relation to the Property. The Owner agrees to pay the fee stated in Section 4.0. The Manager shall have the actual authority set out in Section 3.0, together with the usual and ostensible authority required to perform the said Services.

2.0 Term

2.1 This Agreement shall commence on the Effective Date and shall continue for a period of ___ years ("Initial Contract Period") unless terminated earlier as provided in Section 5.0 hereof.

2.2 This Agreement will automatically renew after the Initial Contract Period for successive periods of twelve (12) months (each referred to as an "Extended Rental Period") on the same terms and conditions until terminated in accordance with Section 5.0 hereof unless either party gives the other no less than ninety days (90 days) written notice prior to the end of the applicable Extended Contract Period that it does not wish to renew the Agreement or wishes to renegotiate any one or more of its terms or conditions.

2.3 The "Term" used in this Agreement shall mean the Initial Rental Period and all Extended Rental Periods.

3.0 Manager's Responsibilities

The Manager agrees to perform the following duties and responsibilities with regard to the Property:

3.1 The Manager shall maintain a Trust Account and name the Owner as the beneficiary for all the money involved in managing the Property.

3.2 The Manager shall advertise the Property for rent, engage and screen prospective tenants, and enter into leasing agreement(s) with the acceptable tenant(s). The Owner shall reimburse the Manager for all expenses related to such Advertising. The Manager shall notify the Owner, in advance, of anticipated expenses related to such Advertising.

3.3 The Manager shall be responsible for paying all the bills for property taxes, insurance, utilities and expenses related to the Property from the Trust Account.

3.4 The Manager shall be responsible for all collection of rent earned on the Property.

3.5 The Manager shall be responsible for all necessary maintenance and repairs to the Property. The Manager shall get the Owner's approval for any expenses exceeding five Thousand Dollars ($5,000) before performing or signing any contract for the repairs. Suppose the repairs or services to be an emergency and the Manager is unable to secure the approval of the Owner in a timely fashion after making commercially reasonable efforts to reach the owner. In that case, the property manager should have the discretion to repair.

3.6 If collection service or legal proceedings become necessary concerning the rental of the Property, the Manager shall handle all such proceedings on behalf of the Owner. The Manager shall not be responsible for any legal proceedings that do not result from the management and rental of the Property.

3.7 The Manager shall prepare and provide a detailed annual report of all rents, expenses, and disbursements to the Owner.

4.0 Compensation

4.1 The Owner agrees to pay the Manager Five Percent (6%) of the net rental income earned in the previous calendar year.

4.2 Payment will be due by Owner to Manager on the 1st of each month based on tenant commitments the preceding month.

4.3 Should the Property be sold during or after the terms of this agreement; this agreement should be assumed by the new owner, or the Owner will pay the fee for the whole term, up to the next renewal date, before the change of the ownership.

5.0 Termination
5.1 This Agreement may be terminated at any time by either Party upon ninety (90) days written notice to the other Party. Upon termination, the Manager shall disburse the Owner any money in the Manager's possession due to the Owner within thirty (30) days from the date of termination.

6.0 Representations and Warranties
6.1 Both Parties represent that they are fully authorized to enter into this Agreement. The performance and obligations of either Party will not violate or infringe upon the rights of any third party or violate any other agreement between the Parties, individually, and any other person, organization, or business or any law or governmental regulation.

7.0 Indemnity
7.1 The Parties each agree to indemnify and hold harmless the other Party, its respective affiliates, officers, agents, employees, and permitted successors and assigns against any and all claims, losses, damages, liabilities, penalties, punitive damages, expenses, reasonable legal

fees and costs of any kind or amount whatsoever, which result from the negligence of or breach of this Agreement by the indemnifying party, its respective successors and assigns that occurs in connection with this Agreement.

7.1 This section shall remain in full force and effect even after termination of the Agreement by its natural termination or the early termination by either Party.

8.0 Limitation of Liability

8.1 Under no circumstances shall either party be liable to the other party or any third party for any damages resulting from any part of this agreement such as, but not limited to, loss of revenue or anticipated profit or lost business, costs of delay or failure of delivery, which are not related to or the direct result of a party's negligence or breach.

9.0 Severability

9.1 In the event any provision of this Agreement is deemed invalid or unenforceable, in whole or in part, that part shall be severed from the remainder of the Agreement, and all other provisions should continue in full force and effect as valid and enforceable.

10.0 Waiver

10.1 The failure by either Party to exercise any right, power, or privilege under the terms of this Agreement will not be construed as a waiver of any subsequent or future exercise of that right, power, or privilege or the exercise of any other right, power, or privilege.

11.0 Legal and Binding Agreement

11.1 This Agreement is legal and binding between the Parties as stated above. The Parties each represent that they have the authority to enter into this Agreement.

12.0 Governing Law and Jurisdiction

12.1 The Parties agree that this Agreement shall be governed by the law of the State, Province, and/or Country in which the Property is located.

13.0 Entire Agreement

13.1 The Parties acknowledge and agree that this Agreement represents the entire agreement between the Parties. In the event that the Parties desire to change, add, or otherwise modify any terms, they shall do so in writing to be signed by both Parties.

The Parties agree to the terms and conditions set forth above as demonstrated by their signatures as follows:

_____   _____

(Manager)   (Date)

_____   _____

(Owner)   (Date)